# Mission Hope

## Thriving Through Seasons of the Soul

# Mission Hope

## Thriving Through Seasons of the Soul

Printed and Electronic Versions
ISBN Paperback: 978-1-956353-42-6
ISBN eBook: 978-1-956353-43-3
(Char Murphy / Motivation Champs)

The book was printed
in the United States of America.

To order additional copies or bulk order contact the publisher,
Motivation Champs Publishing.
www.motivationchamps.com

# Praise for *Mission Hope*

Life is a series of conversations; they become stories weaved together into a tapestry of trials, tribulations, triumphs, and courage. Throughout the pages of this book, you will cry, feel compassion for and perhaps identify with the authors, cheer for success, be inspired, and most of all have hope. The women and men who opened themselves up to share what is raw and real-life experiences have incredible perseverance that is admirable and encouraging for anyone who struggles or has struggled through life's most difficult adversities. This book is a must-read, giving a glimpse into what is possible through a seemingly impossible journey into healing and empowerment.

*Eileen Bild*
*Founder, OTEL Universe*
*A Universal Voice*

Hope can often be found virtually everywhere—sometimes, though, where we least expect it. The stories of those living with dignity in the face of adversity and those who have overcome great difficulties can provide us with the motivation to strive for the best in life.

As I read the accounts of such individuals, I was inspired by the strength and courage they had to face their trials. We don't need to be superheroes to come out victorious, but these stories show us that ordinary people can still achieve what is extraordinary.

*Harry Spaight*
*Author, Selling With Dignity*

This book expanded my world adventure. These inspiring stories are about loss and healing of all kinds as well as Universal Law. There are 18 touching and powerful life-changing stories in this compilation, *Mission Hope*. I highly suggest you read this book, knowing you will reframe your life thereafter.

*Joanne Victoria*
*True Calling Life Coach*
*The Joanne Victoria Group*
*Podcast Host/Author/Speaker*

This book, *Mission Hope,* shares powerful stories which honestly and effortlessly span the physical, emotional, intellectual, and spiritual dimensions, offering the reader a deeply personal glimpse into the multi-level challenges that its 18 authors were presented with from early formative years as well as the life-long lessons they have embraced and learned so much from. Their stories have allowed each one of them to create a mature adult reality of consciously chosen joy and beauty through hope. An inspirational testament to the power of surrender which, when coupled with the sincere and faithful self-effort of the individual, can shine a light on the resilience of the human spirit and help guide others to their rightful place in the circle of life.

*Elizabeth R. Urabe*
*Spiritual Midwife*
*Spirit Art Medium*
*C(osmic) E(nergy) O(rchestrator) at URABE OFFICIAL*

This wonderful and needed collection takes one through many stories of hardship to triumph with fantastic insight and detail. Having suffered huge personal losses all at once, I found this book to be a worthy companion through my own grief and helpful to get on to the healing path. Anybody who has danced in the halls of adversity will find strength in these stories.

Debbie Kasper
*Emmy-nominated writer and award-winning writer performer.*
*International best-selling author, You're Not That Pretty & Other*
*Things My Parents Told Me*

I thoroughly enjoyed reading *Mission Hope: Through Seasons of the Soul*. To say I couldn't wait to get to each chapter is an understatement because this book is amazing! Each chapter is written with compassion, empathy, sensitivity, and understanding. This book demonstrates the ability to advance, despite one's difficulties, and positively affect and make a difference in the lives of others. I could relate, being the mother of a special needs little girl called Maria. Despite obstacles and challenges, hope gives us the impetus to move forward and overcome them. *Mission Hope* can inspire us all.

"When traveling is made too easy and comfortable, its spiritual meaning is lost."

These words of wisdom from D.T. Suzuki, the Japanese-American monk who was instrumental in bringing the Zen philosophy to the West, could have been written by any of the authors in *Mission Hope: Through Seasons of the Soul*. Each and every chapter invites the reader to share their journey through love, loss, and spiritual awakening. With raw honesty, soulful self-awareness, and a belief that love and happiness are our birthright, the authors' messages are a remedy for the turmoil of these times. I invite you to turn the pages and join their unforgettable journeys.

Laura Nadel, Ph.D.
*Author: The Five Gifts: Discovering Hope, Healing, and Strength*
*When Disaster Strikes.*

Life gifts us with poets, writers, storytellers, artists, and troubadours. They are the chosen few, a band of hardcore troubadours that travel the lost highways together. They sit and stare at the blank page at 3 a.m., waiting for the poem to awaken so that it may be unleashed. It will come, maybe not tonight, but the poem and the poet will in time reveal its secrets.

Stories are best when they are shared. We learn by listening and sharing tales of our journey. Each of us has a story to tell, a bit of knowledge to share that will help us along our way. In this book, you will find sadness; you will find joy; the words will touch your heart, inspire you, and make you want more.

This is an amazing book filled with life, love, and living. I would say to you, don't miss this journey written in words from the memories and inspiration of some passionate writers, poets, and storytellers.

*Larry Tyler - Poet, Writer, and Photographer*
*Dirt Road Storytellers*
*The Writers' CafeFeature contributor and columnist for* http://bizcatalyst360.com/

Over the past decade-plus, I've had the unique opportunity to curate thousands of essays, books, and storytelling articles on topics spanning the life, culture, and business spectrum. Mixed among this has been just a handful of non-fiction books naturally destined for best-seller status such as this one. Rarely have I come upon such an extraordinary 'first-person' compilation of stories that will tug at your heart like those found here, borne of remarkable candor and vulnerability. Simply a great read from cover to cover and, for so many, a treasure trove of wisdom discovered.

*Dennis J. Pitocco*
*Publisher & Editor-in-Chief*
*Award-Winning BizCatalyst 360°*

Reading stories in this anthology gives me hope. Hope that people will be more open to sharing 'the whole story' and not just the curated 'holiday letter' highlights. Hope that someone will recognize their own life in one of the stories and know they are still lovable. Hope that the courage these authors show testifies to how vulnerability is not weakness. Let it give you hope too.

*Charlotte Wittenkamp, Bridgebuilder*

# TABLE OF CONTENTS

Angels are Beings
whose Essence has transcended
restrictions of form

Embodying love
with every breath and heartbeat
they abide in peace

Silent witnesses
to the innate perfection
of God's Creation

When penned from a place
of pure, spacious Consciousness...
even words have wings.

—*E.R. Urabe*

# INTRODUCTION

---

## Char Murphy

Within these golden pages, you will find 18 powerful, enlightening, and entertaining stories about Hope and Rising Above Life's Adversities. A timeless book filled with encouragement and inspiration for dealing with the constant changes in a topsy-turvy world spinning around all of us right now. No one is exempt. No one!

I put this book together for you, choosing only 18 of the most inspiring people whom I knew had overcome and risen above the many obstacles that had been laid at their feet. They found the courage and strength, the resilience, to reach down deeper within themselves "to find out who they really are, who they always have been." To love themselves just as they are. And through this process—their journey—their struggles led them here to pass on the wisdom gained through it all to you.

Each of these authors, in their respective ways, has the same vision of helping and supporting humanity during such a critical time in history as we have been and are still going through now. We all came together here to let you know you are not alone in your everyday struggles and heartbreaking circumstances now or ever and that you, as well as all of us here, are, as the famous author and brilliant speaker Wayne Dyer so aptly described it, "spiritual beings having a physical experience." And little did he know when he said those words that cancer would end his life just a few years later.

The time is now for you to step up and into your 'unshakeable power' to find out who you really are and believe in yourself. When the tsunamis of life threaten to destroy you and throw you off balance, you will have the strength, determination, and resilience to fight, keep going, and never give up Hope!

Moreover, these authors have the heart and authenticity to share and bare their souls. Most said they cried all the way through writing and re-living their old stories … because they (we) each have been where you are in one way or another and are writing a new, more powerful story now.

No one has the same story. All of our experiences are unique to each one of us, yours included. After reading this book, it is our greatest desire that you will have the necessary tools to equip yourself with Hope; to stay the course, my friends; and overcome anything you might be faced with. Having overcome their fears and challenges, every one of these authors has written a new script for their life, helping others every day in their unique ways using their special skills and abilities. And now, you're being given the opportunity to do it for yourself.

These 18 amazing authors inspired even me and reminded me to continue keeping Hope alive. I know they will do the same for you too. I am highlighting them all right here. I did not share my own story of overcoming breast cancer four separate times; literally going blind; even now having glaucoma; taking care of my father at the young age of 19, who passed away after five years of fighting and suffering from ALS.

At a later age, I watched helplessly as my beautiful, strong mother died a long, slow death from Alzheimer's. These are both devastating, long-term illnesses that show no mercy to their victims and still have no cure as of this writing. Through all of this and even more, I learned who I truly am, that I am stronger than I ever thought I could be. Now, I empower (in-power) others every day, any way I can, knowing we are all resilient beings just doing the best we can in every moment in these physical bodies. But this book is not about me or my personal story; it's about you and these 18 incredible authors, their stories, and their journeys. You can read more about my story in my book *Unshakeable Power ~ Through Seasons of the Soul,* available on Amazon and published by Motivation Champs, our amazing publisher here.

The chapters and stories you will read now were written by everyday people just like you and me. They range anywhere from overcoming abuse of all kinds: an 18-year-old 'born into chaos' shares in a vulnerable way how she was able to help stop teen suicides; you will hear from an author what it felt like to come out as 'gay' at a young age before it was accepted and how he learned who he truly is beyond the labels; being diagnosed as a schizophrenic and moving through it; losing a job and starting over; managing grief while living with MS; dealing with the recent, devastating loss of a loved one. It's all right here to 'in-power' you.

These authors have each discovered or re-discovered their inner power and strength through hope and found themselves to be their authentic selves, no longer hiding as victims of their circumstances. Each one opens their heart and soul to share nuggets of wisdom and tips to help 'in-power' and inspire each one of you reading. I guarantee you will be able to relate to many, if not all, of them in some way.

Take our hands now as we join together as one to give you hope through faith and love to find joy. Open and read these beautiful stories now to receive and accept these gifts from our hearts to yours. It is our greatest pleasure and joy to serve you, your families, and your friends.

"Time heals all wounds but leaves behind the scars ... only to remind us where we've been and who we really are."

*—Char Murphy, author*

May God bless you all ~ written on behalf of all the authors here.

We are grateful to all of you.

CHAPTER 1

# Return to Love

———

Babien Avila

When I reflect on my journey and ask myself what mattered most and, therefore, hurt the most at that one moment in time when I actually lost them, I realize that it was my husband and my family home. Between Oct. 20th and Nov. 1, 2015, both were snatched away abruptly! Like the proverbial rug yanked out from under any stability I had left in my life or the belief I even had stability at all. Now, to be brutally honest, I knew both could happen at any time, but being the champion compartmentalizer that I was, I also knew that with faith, hope, decisive action, and stoic strength, my dreams of happiness and stability could be achieved.

The denial I was so beautifully captured in had served a clear purpose to help me endure a seemingly endless stream of negative outcomes around my marriage and family life. I had become blind in one eye to this, yet pretty clear in the other during many sleepless nights of tossing and turning with fear and anxiety. What's interesting to me now is that I became nearly blind in my left eye early this year from a cataract until I gratefully had surgery to correct it completely this past summer.

The brain is a marvelous organ. It only lets us feel and see what we can handle at one time, so it's a layered kind of denial that keeps us from going over the edge. I was not ever going to be *that* person. My parents (already deceased at this time) taught me well to be strong in the face of life's disasters and, insanely enough, grow from them.

Shock set in that fateful night when a very distraught young officer knocked on my door around 8:00 p.m. He would give me the most unbelievable news I could not even imagine. "Sit down," he said. All I remembered for weeks after that was my daughter screaming in the house, my journey to the hospital, and arriving in the morgue that night—where we saw my husband lying on a metal table with a trachea tube in his throat. I knew this kind young officer and was so grateful for his ability to get us there safely, despite the dire circumstances facing us. I immediately thought of my son in Japan, studying abroad at the time. How in God's name was I supposed to break the news to him when he was virtually alone in a foreign country? My kids were 17 and 20 at the time.

To be clear, my husband was a wonderful man with a huge heart and a gripping addiction to alcohol and substances. He had been fighting these demons for a while, alongside mental health issues. Luis was a generous and loving man who harbored dark memories that plagued him throughout his shortened life and our marriage. AA helped enormously and delivered seven wonderful sober years of happiness before the snowball again started rolling down the hill. It was not the first time we fought these insidious demons. At the time of his death, we had been married for 21 years.

Prior to his passing, my husband had been in rehab for six weeks and really dealt with much of his despair and rage. Looking back, I guess it was not nearly enough. A chance invitation from an old 'party buddy' while running an errand downtown was the fatal move that led to his death. When I retuned home from work that day with my daughter in tow, we found the front door unlocked, and the TV still on, which was unusual. Clearly, he was only planning on a quick trip close by. This 'friend' apparently offered him a taste of some drug that rendered him unconscious and suppressed his breathing. We found out from the detective on this case that when a patient is clear of substances in their system after a rehab stay, re-introduction of even a tiny amount can suppress their breathing and kill them. This 'friend' was found by the police frantically giving my husband CPR in our parked car after a 911 call. He was still barely alive but had been without oxygen for too long and passed in the emergency room soon after.

I believe he may have given up because, only two weeks before, we were told we had to vacate our home immediately. A judge in our county decided to violate a two-week 'foreclosure stay' as well as ignore a 'short sale' deal that we had with the mortgage company at the time. This deal would have enabled us to sell at a slight profit and move. The judge, instead, without warning and without notifying our lawyer, chose to sell on the auction block for $200,000, less than our deal already in process.

I found this all out only a few hours before because a realtor friend of mine was there at the auction, looking to buy a property that day! I left work from my job in NYC in a panic, stating an 'emergency,' and traveled to the County Courthouse in tears to try and stop the sale. I called my attorney, who never received a 'Notice' of this seemingly illegal sale. I was denied entrance to the Courthouse without my attorney, and by the time he arrived, our house had been sold! This had to be illegal, and I desperately wanted to fight it! But who would step up to take on this judge? NO ONE!

There went our life as we knew it, right down the drain … with everyone standing by, watching. How could this be? We begged for answers … I had been fighting this foreclosure for years because of a contract with a mortgage company that became null and void when the company folded. The bank that took over the loan refused to honor the refinance contract and subsequently went under as well. Seven modification attempts had been denied when we landed a great buyer. All of this time, effort, sweat, and tears for nothing but failure and misery. I had no recourse. At this point, I was completely blindsided and defeated. Disillusioned with the callousness of this action taken against us. Giving up seemed the only option, but I had two wonderful children and a husband who needed me

… I desperately needed some kind of hope.

After my husband died, I was denied life insurance from my job due to the claim that my husband never signed a letter. A letter that we never saw. He was not planning on leaving us and was not suicidal, but he clearly had given up on life. Nothing was going in the right direction for us. We had been fighting a losing battle for so long by the time we realized that selling much sooner might have been a better decision. This all took place during the housing crisis in the US. We were just one of the tragic stories of those who fell through the cracks …

I realized that night that I did not have the luxury of giving up. I still had my two beautiful kids—my daughter in high school with issues of her own and my 20-year-old son studying abroad. I needed to summon up every ounce of strength within me to be there for them, pack up my house, and move to a suitable apartment. I also had to continue working during this time. I begged God and the angels to somehow get me through.

I was in shock but determined. It was my worst nightmare coming to pass … The grieving process would have to wait. I walked through the next week in a haze of nothingness as I planned out the funeral with the help of my in-laws and oldest stepdaughter. The generosity of our friends and the community was incredible. Food mysteriously appeared daily on our porch, along with cards and donations—truly an outpouring of love and support that we will never forget. My Buddhist friends came to chant at our house and invited me to join in, which helped keep me calm enough to navigate the maze of this unbearable nightmare day by day. My son's school made all the arrangements to fly him home from Japan for the funeral to say goodbye to his father, then flew him back to finish his year abroad. This was an amazing gift as well that I will never forget. I took a selfie of the two of us at the airport with our tear-stained faces and 'deer in the headlight' expressions. At this point, I even feared for my son's survival. I felt a gripping fear in my gut about my kids since both my parents were deceased, and I was an only child. They were literally everything to me and all I had left. The trauma that they have suffered is an eerie reminder of losing my own mother when I was still in school so many years ago. You never really get over these kinds of losses. It informs your life so powerfully going forward.

At the wake and funeral service, so many friends, family, and work buddies—as well as teachers from the schools my children attended and church friends, fellow choir members, and clergy—kindly came to pay their respects and shared wonderful stories about my handsome, charismatic, and upbeat husband. Very few knew about his private despair and the demons that haunted him nightly. He would wake up screaming "Get off me!" to unseen terrors in the night fairly often. My daughter and I tearfully sang our last songs to him: "You Raise Me Up" and "Amazing Grace." Then it was done … I felt Lou telling me he was so sorry for leaving us this way at only 53 years old. We had spoken so many times, while sitting on our porch, about the future life we were planning together after the kids were grown and gone. Less stress and more time together. A time that many couples cherish … that would never be.

How exactly was I going to put the shattered pieces of my life together and keep my kids on a safe path forward? I prayed and continued asking for help as I chanted and finally fell asleep crying and exhausted every night, wondering what had become of the life that I had built and asking why.

The packing up and moving house was a blur. So many things never made it to the new apartment. Artwork, chandeliers, bags of clothing, and my husband's tools that we could not fit into the truck the first day were gone from the garage when we came back to pick them up. Stolen after a guarantee they would be safe for a week. Honestly, I was too broken to care at this point. They were just things, but the warm and lovely home we had created was gone for good, with such finality that the three of us have not been able to live together in one place at the same time since. My daughter stayed with me until she graduated and went to college in Ohio for a year, then decided to move to California, which was her dream. My son graduated from college two years later and moved in with me until he took a great job in NYC and got his own apartment. That feeling of family has been torn from us, and we are trying to get it back with short visits. I have also suffered two job losses since and have embarked on a career in spiritual counseling and teaching while still working at my first love singing, songwriting and vocal coaching. I'm also studying to become an RTT therapist to widen the scope of my 'Healing' work. The big dream I have held close to my heart is to purchase and create another home big enough for myself, the kids, and my friends to gather and enjoy together.

Seven years have now passed since the biggest loss in my life, and 'a dark night of the soul' has reared its ugly, yet necessary head for me to reflect on my life and choices, process my grief and confusion, and work on reinventing my life in an honest and authentic way. I want to help others going through trauma or just 'everyday' life, and I am doing this through my spiritual counseling (healing work) and creative musical work—singing and songwriting. Self-healing and meditation practice as well as exercise and diet have also been paramount on my journey toward wellness. My faith in the Divine, the angels, my guides, and especially God our Creator has kept me from despair and self-pity. There are still some days when the grief floods back in. It's a long, hard process. Creating peace and a feeling of well-being and safety on my own has also been a very important goal and has helped me stay healthy physically, mentally, and emotionally. I had very little peace during the last nine years of my marriage, and that trauma has taken its toll, of course, yet, at the same time, it is the very thing that inspires and motivates me to help my clients heal and navigate their way through traumatic life experience in order to find happiness and purpose again. Meditation with music has really been a lifesaver for me as well as daily walks in nature, deep breathing, and Chi Gong techniques. I have found spiritual salt and essential oil baths and massage, as well as Reiki and energetic healing, to be very helpful as well. Spending time with friends and loved ones laughing out loud, singing, and dancing (especially salsa). "Thank you, Luis, for all those wonderful memories of us dancing … they will always raise my vibrational frequency and feelings of joy!"

I want to say to you reading this now: Never lose hope and do what you love! In closing, I want to leave you with a song I wrote titled "Return to Love" (copyrighted). I hope you will enjoy it!

**Return to Love** *by Babien Avila*

*Sometimes sittin' on a mountain doesn't do it*
*It takes us away from those who care*
*But sharing a little kindness and understanding*
*Can give us the capacity to share*

*We've got to return to love*
*Got to return to grace*
*Need to depend on love*
*In order to find our place*
*Got to return to peace, forgive ourselves*
*Then maybe the fighting will cease*

*Time is running out on selfish motives*
*No longer can we close our eyes to pain*
*If we listen to our hearts, then He will tell us*
*How to give your love so everyone will gain*

*We've got to return to love*
*Got to return to grace*
*Need to depend on love in order to find our place*
*Got to return to peace, forgive ourselves*
*Then maybe the fighting will cease*

*The darkness all around will be made light*
*The hardened hearts of bitter years grow soft*
*A miracle can happen throughout the night*
*A new dawn brings forgiveness within our tears*

*As we-e-e-e walk along that road, we may stumble and fall*

*But the secret of tomorrow lies in standing tall*
*With love in our hearts and peace on our minds*
*Let's turn up the volume in our lives*

*We've got to return to love*
*Got to return to grace*
*Need to depend on love in order to find our place*
*Got to return to peace, forgive ourselves*
*Then maybe the fighting will cease*
*Then maybe the fighting will cease*
*You've got to know how to return to love right now—right now.*

*— Babien Avila, 1992*

## About Babien Avila

Babien is a spiritual counselor, divine angel channel, healer, and astrologer. She is also a singer and published songwriter who uses music and sound in her healing practice. From a young age, she was blessed with spiritual gifts of clairaudience, clairsentience, as well as clairvoyance. Babien studied mediumship and became an ordained minister in NYC in the 1990s. She also enjoyed a successful music career recording, performing, and touring. Babien was guided by spirit to start using music as a healing modality in her writing as well as counseling practice and is currently studying to become a licensed RTT therapist to expand her practice of healing and counseling. She is also trained in accessing the 'Akashic Records' for past life related healing and block clearing. Babien's mission is to uplift, heal, and guide those at a crossroads in their lives who have become stuck in patterns or lost faith in their path forward due to challenges, trauma, or crisis and are on a healing journey to create a life of joy and live their highest purpose.

CHAPTER 2

# Love Gives Us Hope

———

### Maria Lehtman

"A tower of sandy rocks, smooth-surfaced, walls reaching for the skies. Flames glowing inside. The heat stalked me through the window openings. Shunned from within as if a stranger to my inner self."

—*Maria Lehtman, The Round Tower Dream, Dew Drops (2013)*

Several years ago, my creative world, a cornerstone of my identity, fell apart. I was utterly unprepared for it, as my essence is founded on the ability to retain and share hope through creative projects. It was not only writer's block. Instead, the eternal flame in my soul that fueled my creativity was almost extinguished. Before we reflect on what broke my most significant source of hope, let me take you on a little journey.

*Where did my flame of creativity begin?* I am a child of the '70s—a decade that I consider a transition to the technology transformation that filled the following decades. It was the last age of innocence when children could still be children without being heavily impacted by peer and brand pressure. Looking back at my childhood pictures, I see that I am wearing handed-down clothing from my male cousins and friends and cute little dresses sewn by my mother. I was utterly unaware if my clothing was 'chic.' The content of life was far more important than the content in media.

The '70s was also, in many ways, the start of a methodological approach to alternative lifestyle hacks. My parents were eager to study self-improvement and healing approaches and include the whole family on that journey. And so, I found myself sitting in a transcendental meditation retreat in Norway with my older sister when I was only five years old. Given my young age, my meditation sessions were only 10 minutes long. We would continue the meditation practice for several years at home. I would sit cross-legged on the floor next to my mother, take note of the time, and slip away after 10 minutes to continue my play.

My mother was especially interested in psychology and pedagogical ways of raising and working with children. Her bedroom always looked like someone had offloaded the library bus around the bed. The only books she did not touch were science fiction—the genre that ironically became my favorite growing up. I had an aptitude for learning, so she encouraged me to develop my skills long before I went to school. As a result, I did math, reading, drawing, and writing, coupled with learning English as my second language, before I turned six. Sports were encouraged, but we spent so much time playing outdoors that we focused more on cognitive learning.

I especially loved reading and drawing—there were no rules to how much imagination I could use to create stories. Unfortunately, I often had horrid nightmares, so I spontaneously banished them during the day, keeping my mind occupied with positive hobbies. The spring of creativity!

"Spring has kept me waiting. Yet, through the rain and seemingly endless clouds, a ray of sunlight escapes."

—*Maria Lehtman, Spring, Dew Drops (2013)*

As soon as I entered school, my writing and reading started in earnest. I enjoyed inventing stories and writing essays, especially related to nature. Geography and languages were my favorite topics. I soon turned to poetry and scribbled nature poems in my notebooks with little illustrations and stickers. For many years, I imagined growing up and being an author and an artist. My mother encouraged me to write more and even enrolled me in a famous poetry retreat.

Little did I know that my approach to writing was considered 'whimsical.' I was the youngest in the seminar, 11 years old. I was hardly going to write about broken hearts, nights with empty wine bottles, and the grimness of life and relationships. That seminar shook off some of my confidence. How would I ever be a creative talent if all I could write about was nature and supernatural beings (fairies and elves)? My inner world was looking for beauty in the world, despite the challenges we faced growing up.

On the positive side, the seminar also made me consider what art was. It could be anything. An everyday utensil like a teaspoon we use today might be the most remarkable historical art discovery a thousand years forward. If art could be anything, who was to say my 'whimsical' writing style was not just as good as anyone else's? My mother continued to call me her little poet girl, and I kept writing about how I perceived nature, with or without imaginary beings.

A few years later, my mother discovered a new passion: the study of dreams. As an avid dreamer, I was thrilled to learn more about them. We found a whole new universe to explore together. I would tell her significant dreams of mine, and she would help me unlock their secrets. So, I started to write dream journals, and these weird mythical worlds became my new passion. We would have hours and hours of inspirational sessions with my mother sharing dreams and pondering about life from its many angles. Some of our discussions were even spiritual because we both firmly believed our lives had a more significant meaning. Our dream dialogues explored the unconscious—our true identities, hidden fears, desires, and capabilities. I firmly believed I would write a book about dream interpretation one day. Who would not want to break the cycle of nightmares and understand the meaning of what seemed like bad dreams and were actually about personal transformation?

**The parallel life of harsh reality**

*Today*
*I long for the small thoughts*
*Like dew drops on a sleeping fern*
*Or a pearl of water*
*Balancing on the silent*
*Riverstone's brow -*
*There for a moment*
*But soon dissolved*

—*Maria Lehtman, Small Thoughts, Dew Drops (2013)*

Most of us have been there. Our childhood dreams get washed away by the sheer realities of life. Bills must be paid, and money earned for food and everyday living. I still hoped to be an artist but needed more time to study, work, and apply for colleges with art majors. The seats were limited, and requirements were extremely high. I came close once on a waiting list, but I realized I was better off continuing my studies for travel and trade to get a job. For a young, adventurous woman, working for the travel industry was a dream job—well, for anything but the pay. However, I was financially capable of getting married as well as able to travel, have a car, and see the world with my husband. My artistic vision hovered further away with every passing year.

When the airline industry started to see one recession after another, I changed to the IT world. My mother was happy with my progress and my ability to keep traveling. We lived in different cities, but I kept writing to her and visiting her whenever possible. My mother's health had been vulnerable for over a decade by then. She had dramatic ups and downs during the years. Yet, she was so resilient that we tended to say that our mother had 'nine lives.'

I remember a winter day when my mother was diagnosed with an unknown growth in her lungs and drifted rapidly away from us. The tests were painful, and by the third one, she refused them. Finally, she fell into a coma. I panicked. I was not ready for her to die. She was not just my mother but also my soul sister, intrigued by the unknown worlds beyond our reach. I was so terrified about her passing that I shared my fears with a colleague. I considered him a friend, and that he was. He listened to my worries about my mother nearing death. Then he said the words I never forgot: "Do you not think your mother deserves your hope?" Hope. That word echoed in my mind, and I realized how selfish it was for me to delve into my greatest fear. Our mother deserved my support, my hope, and my healing thoughts. So I altered my approach and began sending her positive thoughts, hoping for what was best for her and wishing she would recover.

A miracle happened. The mystical tumor in my mother's lung began to heal. None of the doctors knew what it was or how it disappeared. The illness weakened my mother's condition significantly, but she could gradually move on and continue her life. She later described her experience while in a coma. She was looking at a brightly illuminated door in a corridor when her mind drifted away. Then she heard a voice that said: "You may enter if that is your wish, but you still have experiences and meaning in your life if you choose to continue." So, once more, she decided to continue.

It was one of the greatest lessons of hope. I had finally found the cornerstone of my creativity and passion: to share hope. The little beauties in life I had written about were not whimsical at all—they were the very essence of positivity we all needed. Now, all I required was a method to bring my dreams alive.

### When the stars align

*These are my colors -*
*The mixtures of brown, gold, and copper.*
*The sun lazily over the horizon -*
*The sea restless,*
*Waiting for the roar of winds.*

*The first autumn storm.*
*Not yet, I know -*
*Today everything is bright.*

—Maria Lehtman, *My Colours, Dew Drops (2013)*

Not long after the digital innovations tide turned toward consumers, I was finally able to buy my first digital camera, and I picked up photography in earnest. My little hobby grew into a passion. In 2006, I opened my own business aside from my daily work. It was extremely satisfying to create, write, and discover the enormous possibilities of digital art. Before social media influencers became the norm, I knew that digital imagery would change the perception of art. Being an artist would no longer be an exclusive club. Creating art was available and affordable to anyone with internet access and a mobile device.

The digital age finally allowed people with many talents to advance and gain acceptance in international communities. Art and creativity should always be about empowerment, not about exclusion. My interest in photography and graphic design was about something other than earning money. I created designs about everything I loved as a child: beauty, hope, and inspiration from nature. I wanted to share the fantastic stories of our beautiful Earth with as many people as possible.

As passionate as I was about my work in IT, the hours wore me out after seven years. My physiology was completely confused from working in two, sometimes three, continental time zones. To my credit, I had survived the pace much longer than many of my male colleagues. My mind was sharp, but my body was—as my acupuncture therapist said—like armor. She was lucky to get any needles in place without me trying to squiggle away from the pain. As much as I hated to admit it, my health could no longer endure the strain.

I had to stay on sick leave for an extended period to recover. It allowed me to look back and consider where I was headed. I was blessed to find another job in IT, but one with much more personal growth potential and a culture where I could be myself. Who had I been before that? It felt that I had done everything expected of me at work, and it had turned me away from my natural, empathic behaviors. The light in me felt all but extinguished.

During my recovery months, I gradually started to feel hope again. My mother constantly asked me about developing my artistic skills. So, when my sister established her own business, I thought, *Why not?* I launched a web shop for my designs and poetry. I made enough money to cover my equipment and the software I needed. I created, designed, and inspired customers and felt more alive than I had in years. My new employer was understanding and allowed me to keep my company while I kept working my day job.

My goal was to help people see the beauty in the world. Brands had become disassociated from nature, and I wanted to bring it back to them as a soft branding alternative. Who would not want to see their story described through the beauty of the thousands of lakes and forests we have in our country? People needed inspiration, authentic values, and visions they could personally relate to. The power of transformation!

"We should never let go of our dreams because they will never give up on us."

—*Maria Lehtman*

Fast forward seven years. I realized I had spent all this time with my passion enterprise, and most of my time went into operational up-keeping. However, my dream of creating a book still needed to be realized. My family kept asking me about publishing a book, given that I had over 100,000 photographs and designs in my archives by then. So, with a heavy heart, I closed down my art business and, within a year, published my first photographic and poetic journey book.

No other creative project had ever felt as easy as designing my authentic poetry-photography journey from scratch. I have served many happy customers during my years. Still, nothing compared to the genuine delight of my loved ones when they received my freshly printed books.

My writing facets opened up, and I started writing posts, blogs, and articles accompanied by my pictures. I wrote about my discoveries during our travels; the beauty of nature; how to overcome personal challenges; self-transformation; and the necessity to stay authentic to ourselves, no matter what, and keep connected with the Earth.

I wanted people to see through my eyes how I felt the peace surrounding me in the national parks. After a short walk through the evergreen woods or by the ocean, I always came back feeling refreshed—as if someone had dusted me off and inserted a jewel in my heart. I sensed hope again. By then, my mother had long since retired and could no longer use a computer. So, I printed out every blog and either mailed them to her or took them with me when I visited her. Of course, we always sat down to discuss what thoughts came to her mind when she read them.

I created a weekly habit of sending her postcards and writing letters with poetry. She kept asking me to save my poems for publishing later on. But, I confess, I only preserved part of them. It was not about creating a legacy for me but seeing how her face brightened when we discussed the topics. She was in so much pain for most days that it was nice to take her mind off it, even if for a few moments.

We also still shared dreams, and I kept my dream journals. Gradually, the tables turned, and my mother came to me more often for advice than I did to her. Then one day, she looked at me and said: "And the student has become the teacher." I felt odd pride about that, but I also knew I owed it all to her. She was the one who had taught me how to swim in the subconscious waters of dreamworlds. There was only one thing she could not teach me: how to manipulate them. I had to learn that by myself. Little did I know that my greatest challenge was yet to come—the first November snow.

"The touch of winter on the grass is like a footprint of an angel—
ever elusive, frail, and yet, clear and promising."

—*Maria Lehtman, Seasons, Dew Drops (2013)*

One late fall night, I saw a dream where I was walking peacefully across a large park. The first snow had just fallen as it usually does in late November. The weather was not sunny nor cloudy—just light. Suddenly, my mother appeared next to me. She did not look much older than me. We talked and felt a pleasant belonging. After a while, she said her goodbyes and faded away.

I woke up and knew what I had seen. My mother let me know she was passing away but wanted to leave me feeling calm about it. I also knew that it would happen at exactly that time of the year—only I did not know what year. The mother I had seen in my dream was confident, healthy, and happy. In contrast, my mother, in the waking world, was torn between life and death. Her chronic pains were increasing, but she loved her family too much to leave us and was utterly fearful about death.

I wanted to create a path of safety and light for my mother to return home. So I combined everything I had learned about energy healing, meditations, and positive association with my creative work and designs. We both believed strongly in life beyond death, but somehow I had to convince her that it was all right to let go and that she would never be far from us.

I admit I pushed my mother out of her comfort zone many times. However, I also knew she woke up every day thanking God for being here with her family and asking mercy to take her back. She grew ever more fragile, and her temperament changed so much that I only recognized her in her text messages and short glimpses of our conversations. Yet, despite her pain, she still reached for her coloring pens and kept drawing little flowers and characters for everyone in our family. She read newspapers, magazines, and books until she could no longer hold them in place. I was unsure if the pure will of life or fear of death kept her with us. Probably both.

Three years after my dream, we learned that my mother had very advanced Alzheimer's. We were all in shock, but we finally understood the dramatic change in her personality. She vehemently denied it. After all, she had always been such a great study—and prided on her excellent memory. Three weeks after the diagnosis, I visited my mother. Her mind was always full of fears, issues, and things that needed to be done in a certain way. But she had brief moments of fluidity. That day, she looked at me and said: "I am no longer afraid." That was it. No further discussion, but I knew exactly what she meant, and I felt relief.

A few months later, when I was with her, she sat on her bed and started saying goodbyes. It was not unusual. She had given her speech of love to my sisters and me many times over the past few years. The unique thing about this time was that she allowed me to film her on my mobile. Usually, whenever she saw that I recorded anything, she changed the topic or just fell silent. I was grateful to capture this beautiful memory of her—through the soul gates.

> "Be not afraid of the door into the unknown. The love and light
> passed on awaits you."
>
> —*Maria Lehtman, The Beyond, The Dreaming Doors (2018)*

And so, the November in my dream came. One dark winter evening, my mother had a stroke and was rushed to the hospital. By the time I visited her, she was already unconscious due to pneumonia and sepsis, and the inner bleeding had not stopped. In 2019, we were still not restricted by the pandemic, so our family, children, and grandchildren gathered in the hospital room for her final hours. We had a wonderful nurse who supported us and let us stay as long as we wanted. She made everyone feel comfortable, and we greatly appreciated her professionalism and care.

The last months before we reached this point had been like a bad dream. Every time we left our mother alone for the night, it felt like we were leaving a helpless child alone. She was so fragile she could barely get from one room to another, and Alzheimer's confused her mind. She had an emergency health service but refused to wear the bracelet, so we were unsure if she would get help on time.

Sitting in the hospital room and looking at her, I struggled to hold back my tears. Yet, having followed her combat all the odds for decades, I felt relief. I knew this would be her final journey, and she would be safe, released from her enormous pain. I prayed for heavenly guides to support her return to the home of light. I placed a healing crystal by her bedside. She used to always carry one with her. I held my husband's hand and looked at my mother; I was blessed with a feeling of complete peace.

I could not stay for the entire night that we knew would be her last. After eight hours, my body was weary, and I had a monstrous migraine when I woke up to my sister's call at night. I stayed home, hardly able to move or breathe through the pain. Yet, I also felt that my journey with her was complete. The long winter of the soul.

"Hope is a light that finds you when you least expect it."

—*Maria Lehtman*

If someone had told me that my mother's passing would shock me, I would not have believed them. Sadness—yes, grief, loneliness—but this utter mental disarray was new to me. The only way to help our family prepare for the memorial services was by taking calls from my bed and lying down. I could spend short moments on the PC taking care of the necessary paperwork sent my way. My nervous system was utterly haywire.

It is an odd conflict that when another person dies, and we most need solitude, we must focus on sorting out their worldly possessions, paperwork, and whatnot. I tried to pitch in as much as I could. My husband did a lot of the heavy lifting for me. After the apartment was empty, I just let go. I continued to take photographs and little walks outside. After the New Year, I returned to work, but my body was only partially healed. I knew it would pick up eventually, and working gave me a necessary rhythm for the days.

I had always thought that my chronic illness would ease when my mother passed away—after all, our worry for her had been constant. But, instead, it took a turn for the worse. Even scarier was the impact on my mind and my heart. I felt depleted and drained. I felt as if someone had opened a faucet in my soul and poured half of it away. The winter was not only outside—the darkness was inside me. The hope I was so used to sharing with others had vanished. There was no creativity left in me.

I realized, for the first time in my life that behind all my creative projects, the driving and energizing force had been my mother. I wanted so much to let her live her dreams through me. So, when people asked me about publishing my next book, I struggled to find words for why I could not create a book or anything for that matter.

Nothing about my shock made sense to me. I had encouraged my mother to look further, to explore the light of the universe, and to trust that we had a future beyond this life. All her life, my mother had depended on her childhood faith; so, ultimately, I only needed to encourage her to keep up and grow that light within her. Yet, with all my knowledge, it seemed like the universe had failed me.

Months went by, but I could not get her passing from my mind; it felt like a cold stone in my heart and soul. I had learned and studied everything I could about energy healing and working with my guides. But, in the end, my feelings betrayed me.

### When does your spring arrive?

*When there is time*
*The time travels*
*To have it as your friend*
*You need to travel on it*

*Stand still*
*Let it flow*
*Feel the currents*
*Resist the pull*
*And then*
*Close your eyes*
*And let go*

—*Maria Lehtman, Time to Let Go, The Dreaming Doors (2018)*

One question I would encourage people never to ask someone is: "Where are you in your grieving process?" It is as utopian a question as death itself. I am familiar with the five stages of grief in theory—sometimes called the DABDA model: denial, anger, bargaining, depression, and acceptance. A process requires steps and transitions, even if they are non-linear. All I had was one crashed drive in my emotional stack, and there was nothing to process because it was empty. I was in shock.

There is also no specific timeline for grief. Each of us copes with losses differently. What matters is that we identify what brings us closer to healing and provides us hope to continue. What did I do when I realized there was no fast track for me? I knew I had one element that was on my side: time. If I persisted long enough, repeating creative steps even when I had anything barely to reach for, eventually, the healing process would win.

I started with the basics: baby steps. First, I continued my online presence on social media and posted my photography with little poems or quotes. I did so as often as I could. Not just because I knew it brought hope to others but because it was the only way to retain my creativity. Secondly, I thought about my mother somewhere in the stars and promised I would not give up. Thirdly, I programmed my healing to be processed during the night, in my dreams—after all, I saw dreams of my mother constantly. My concern was that as I could not cry, I might risk suffering a more prolonged trauma. Crying is healing, but it immediately triggered my chronic migraine. I had no sufficient medication for it, so it was not an option.

A good friend said that the first year would be the hardest, the celebrations and festivities. She was right, but it was more the little things I missed. The daily photos and hellos via text messages with my mother. When I saw something beautiful or cute, I immediately snapped a picture and sent it to her. She could not go out much, so in every town I visited, I took photographs for her and sent a postcard or bought a little souvenir. Now, all these little daily traditions were gone.

When spring arrived, my sister helped me plant pansies, or violets, on our terrace. My mother's name means violet, so I always bought some for Mother's Day (during May in Finland). I felt the flowers on our porch were a better place to remember her than visiting her grave. She told me so in a dream. She understood that I was reluctant to visit the graveyard. I just felt she was not there.

During the summer, we took little road trips with my husband, and I kept reaching for postcards and my phone and felt sad every time I realized there wasn't anyone to read them. My thoughts were heavy, and while everything might have seemed all right outside, my mind did not heal. My family would look at old photographs and messages from my mother. I tucked everything away, apart from one or two pictures of her.

My spring did not arrive the next year or the year after. My health dived again, and it took me a few months to figure out how to get back on my feet. While I felt that my well of inspiration was still empty, I kept writing poems. We may have a stardust in our soul that stays protected, no matter what we go through. Our higher consciousness never abandons us.

### The summer arrives

*In the tumult of our lives*
*Are pockets of mystery*
*Sparks emanating from*
*Our very souls*
*Intertwined and pulsing*
*As if small stars*
*Occupied the darkness*
*Within us*
*Behind the solid*
*Near-impenetrable doors*
*Of our hearts*
—*Maria Lehtman, Stargazers, The Dreaming Doors (2018)*

Time, the champion and enemy of life, is relentless. As I am writing this, it is November again. The third year after my mother's passing. I am finally beginning to feel like myself again. My creative light has returned. I am toying with a new poetry book idea, although I am in no hurry. My passion for writing is quite different, yet, now, my writing has a purpose. I dedicate this story to all of you who have lost dear ones. I want you to know that you are not alone and that time can work miracles if you let it. Grief has no specific shape or form. The range of feelings varies from one person to another. Therefore, it is essential to accept your emotions and recognize them, even if there are none. You might feel completely numb.

I will never be the same person I was. No one ever is when they face great sorrows and challenges. I have much more respect for the human body now. Even if I learn to build the most brilliant coping mechanisms, I cannot stop what ultimately happens in my physiology. Our lives are much larger and more complicated ecosystems than we understand. While my mind had worked on my mother's transition for years, the impact hit me because her death tore apart the fabric of our connected lives. Our energy is not without bounds.

The bonding between people is real. The more sensitive you are, the more emotions you draw from other people around you. As an energy healer, I build even more intricate and comprehensive connections with people I want to support. Toward the end of my mother's journey, I had to stop touching her. Without realizing it, she drew in energy from me to help her, and because of our close connection, I could not withhold it. Physical contact was only a tiny part of our shared interfaces. I am no longer angry with the universe for causing my dramatic shock. It was the price I paid to support my mother in her final journey. I walked that path with my dear family, each of us taking some burdens. If I were given a choice, even knowing the outcome, I would do it all over again.

**Love is all, and hope will give us love!**

## About Maria Lehtman

 Maria Lehtman lives in the Nordics, Finland. She has over 20 years of sales, marketing, and professional services experience from the international telecommunications and travel industry. Her achievements include successful global transition, transformation, and competency programs in management roles in the global telecommunication field. She is currently working in International Sales & Marketing department with the transversal employee and executive social media engagement development programs.

Maria is passionate about digital empowerment and the opportunities it can provide for people worldwide. She is a dedicated photographer and digital artist engaged in several creative projects at any given time. She is a compassionate leader; her mission is to support people in self-transformation and in embracing new skills. Her trademark is her capability to share a smile, even during the most challenging circumstances, and keep a 'mindfulness' attitude.

Maria is a featured contributor and a columnist at the award-winning new media agency BizCatalyst 360˚. Maria's posts and thoughts represent her view of the world. Maria is a contributing author to two inspiring books published by Sacred Stories. She has also published two poetic photography journey books: *Dew Drops* and *The Dreaming Doors - Through the Soul Gateways*. She is focused on sharing beauty, inspiration, love, and hope through her writing.

Poem references:

*Dew Drops: The Round Tower Dream, Spring, Seasons*

Author page on Amazon: www.amazon.com/author/marialehtman
Amazon: Maria's publications: *Hiljainen Hetki (Dew Drops)* and *The Dreaming Doors*
Sacred Stories collaboration: *Chaos to Clarity: Sacred Stories of Transformational Change* and *Crappy to Happy Sacred Stories of Transformational Joy*
Columnist: www.bizcatalyst360.com/author/marialehtman/
Website: www.thedigitalteacup.com
Instagram: @thedigitalteacup
Twitter: @LehtmanMaria
LinkedIn: https://fi.linkedin.com/in/marialehtman

CHAPTER 3

# Reclaiming Value(s)

––––

Susan LePlae Miller

"Hope keeps our head above water
when the storms are raging around us.
Hope anchors us with strength to overcome life's challenges.
Hope is a sail to bring us to new possibilities.
Hope believes in you.
Believe in Hope."

—*Susan LePlae Miller*

Every person wants to feel seen, heard, and understood for who they actually are—even if they don't realize it. This feeling of love, acceptance, and hope comes more naturally when we're young. We see it in the stars and clouds and in the buckets of sticks, grass, and berries we gather in the backyard. We hear it in the sounds of our loved ones' voices; in the birds chirping; and in the rivers, lakes, and streams. It's a feeling that penetrates our senses and has an understanding all its own. The world has a certain wonder, and we feel it in everything we do and are.

Painful moments can chip away at our wonder. It is as though pieces of who we are float away, and we don't even realize it's happening until they disappear behind the clouds, sight unseen. Life then begins to compile a seriousness upon us that we weren't prepared for until we feel almost foolish for having ever been content with simplicity. Maturity beckons us with rules, expectations, assumptions, and comparisons while we dutifully apply each layer. And soon, the ease and flow we once knew is almost forgotten and can be hard to reclaim when we feel lost in the commotion of battle and survival.

Joyful moments offer glimpses of our childhood selves, although we don't always give them the proper attribution. Our lives bounce back and forth as we take on more responsibility while the sun rises and sets with or without our awareness. On occasion, we feel a sense of exhilaration as we notice the magic peeking above the horizon and through the clouds. For a moment, we breathe in the possibility of something we can't quite recall, but with each of life's complications, we forget again and offer the silver lining to the clouds themselves and not to the light of what we once held dear. Soon a word, sight, or sound is given the power to trigger our joy and pain. The less aware we become, the more we try to rationalize our reactions as we over-think, plan, and process our survival. Rather than live, we seek to get-by; we seek to survive. Survival and success become mistakenly interwoven, while a feeling of freedom is left behind.

This is where my story begins, unaware, getting-by. Love, acceptance, and hope had been clouded over, and I didn't have the tools to unleash myself from my own prison. Yes, I had survived and succeeded in many ways, but I didn't know how to live, and it would take decades to finally break through.

One of my first awareness awakenings began in my thirties during a weekend retreat. As a working-mother, I was exhausted and ready for a weekend away. I had no inkling of what would come from this experience other than a break. The facilitator asked us to map out our lives and to look at the cycles of change we remembered, both good and bad. It had been years since I thought, consciously, about some of these experiences. Many were buried under layers of intentional forgetfulness. Once the flow of thoughts began, the highs and lows appeared with hills, valleys, rapids, and still water.

Ages 5, 6, 11, 12, 17, 18, 19: each of these ages held painful memories, moments that chipped away at my childhood essence. Of course, I had joy, just not in ways that would show up on this map. The valleys leveled before hills appeared: 26, 29, 31, 32, 34. The hills brought new pieces and dimensions to my life. We sectioned off our life maps and looked at the details more closely for additional clues as to how and when we had changed. Until then, I hadn't been intentionally conscious of how instances from early childhood had altered my existence. By the end of the weekend, I was emotionally exhausted with a deeper recognition of when and where pieces of myself had changed. It had been decades since I had brought details out from behind the clouds, and I needed extra time alone to process myself back before returning home. I couldn't stuff it all back in but wanted to regain my composure enough and 'put on a good face.'

As a wife, mother of four, and the youngest of six children growing up, my emotional energy was often spread out into what was happening around me. I felt a certain responsibility to be cognizant of how others felt while intentional with my choice of words. I often felt the weight of the world with each of my choices and focused on how I could make a difference for others while leaving my own feelings tucked away inside. Sometimes they exploded without my awareness. The life map exercise from the retreat confounded me, as it was the first time I had ever focused on my own journey. It would not be the last. Throughout the years, I would attend more retreats and dive deeper into myself, but each time, I would try to leave most of myself at the door as I returned home. It would take more than a weekend away to bring myself home again. And so, the journey continued, with the recognition of a few adulthood experiences that shifted my perspective enough to finally bring me home.

One of the most memorable adult shifts happened on September 11th, 2001. Many of us vividly remember this day. It was a Tuesday. I remember precisely where I was when the call came in on my cell phone as I was driving into the office, with our three youngest children in their car seats;

my husband had dropped our oldest off for kindergarten. As I pulled up to a traffic light, my cell phone rang, and life changed with these words: "Turn on the radio; something terrible just happened. A plane flew into the World Trade Center!"

Prior to that moment, I was focused on a career that was flourishing with promotions and travel while also managing a family with four children ages five and under. I was valued at work and fortunate to have a hybrid work schedule before it was even 'a thing.' This particular day, that phone call and moment in time changed everything. Our daycare was on the first floor of our office building, and I was filled with fear of the unknown. *What's going to happen next? Are our schools safe? Is our daycare safe? Would a car come blasting through the windows? How can I go upstairs to my office?*

Never before had these thoughts entered my mind, as I had taken for granted the regularity of my adult life. The time for apathy was over. Over the next few days, we spoke with our small children about what was happening in the world and made decisions as a family that would impact life as we knew it. You might think our children were too young to know the difference, but they knew things were not right, and we did our best to help them understand. I was on track for another promotion when I walked into my manager's office and requested a lay-off since our company was gearing up for another round. This was no easy decision. I'm a first-generation college graduate and had grown up in a divorced household as the youngest of six children. My psychological safety net of independence and autonomy was now at risk. I knew, even before I left my job, the return to the workforce would be a challenge.

Many who take a career break risk derailing their career and never return to the same income level or job title. We experienced this very thing again during the COVID pandemic in 2020. The road back to my own career was riddled with challenges that inspired my mantra: "Know your value; live your values."

But this was 2001, and I did what every Type-A career, now stay-at-home, mom would do. I encouraged my husband to get his master's and got involved in making sure our children would have the love and support we felt they needed at school, church, and in their activities. If no one volunteered to run or participate in a committee or group, I would do it. From being Mother's Club president to a Couple's Bible Study leader, to the PTO volunteer coordinator and Ways and Means chair, those early years were full, and my project management skills did not get stale; in fact, they grew stronger.

One of the biggest differences in paid versus volunteer work is a lack of financial incentives and a lack of acknowledgment from the working world of the experiences themselves. Volunteers need to be inspired, motivated, or appreciated in another way because the financial model of reward is not available. Together, with my fellow volunteers, we learned to tap into our creativity and collective experiences to get the jobs done. A resume that once contained million- and billion-dollar work experiences now contained a long list of other accomplishments that were life-altering in a different way. This shift in understanding taught me to look beyond the resume when seeking future employees and coworkers and to listen more intently to how values were infused into the actions of future employers and partners. Action truly does speak louder than words.

As our children got older, I shifted to more philanthropic volunteer positions and felt the call to create a Jean Drive through St. Vincent de Paul in order to give people a solid and more sustainable piece of clothing each autumn. The Jean Drive was inspired by how I felt as a teenage girl, craving the Calvin Klein designer jeans my friends wore while knowing it was not in our budget to purchase them. Now, as an adult, I was in a position where we could buy our kids many things while also recognizing not everyone was able to do so. My business skills were put to good use on the logistical and marketing challenges, and the community was generous with their donations. Together, we distributed over 11,000 pairs of jeans to those in need, with no cost to the nonprofit or clients we were serving. Hidden value, bursting with values, filled the crevices of my experience as I learned the importance of offering programs with compassionate care and dignity for the client at every step of the way.

Through these years, our children played sports, participated in activities, did well in school, and my husband and I enjoyed seeing them flourish while we helped to run Booster Clubs and community events. Eventually, I started to work again, but the transition back was a challenge just as I had expected. While my skills were enhanced with new experiences, they were not necessarily valued in the job market or on my resume, so the 'comeback' was slow. I prioritized positions where I would be available to attend as many of our children's activities as possible while growing new skillsets to adapt to the constant technological changes in the workplace.

By the end of 2019, with two college graduates and our two youngest in college, I was ready for something more and different. It was time to shift the focus back to my own career, but new challenges were abundant. It was hard to remember what my own interests were. Sure there were many things I could do, but what did I want to do? In addition, I could feel the weight of the political climate on friends, family, and acquaintances, as the news and social media were filled with a bitter contentious divide. Simultaneously, my work environment was out of alignment with my values, and most Monday mornings began in tears. It would take the whole week to rebuild myself again, as my confidence waned. Did I really work this hard to feel like this at this time in my life? I felt demoralized, degraded, and depressed. The only voices I could hear, shut me down even further. I appeared to 'have it all,' and yet I felt as though I was starting over again.

> *What do you have to complain about?*
> *Others have it a lot harder than you.*
> *You don't have to work.*
> *At least you're healthy.*
> *Put on a good face.*
> *Your life is perfect.*
> *You had a choice.*

---

*You're so lucky.*
*It's just a job.*
*Cheer up.*
*Smile.*

I heard those words over and over, sometimes from the outside in; other times, from the inside out. Each statement made me feel more invisible and more alone, prolonging the guilt, blame, shame, and sadness. It became easier to say less, feel less, do less, be less, and stop trying. At some point, I started to believe that burying the pain would make it easier to appear as though I were fine, just like I did while dealing with (or not dealing with) my childhood challenges.

Of course, I was fortunate in many ways, and a new level of awareness struck me. While feeling as low as I could remember, I also became compelled to start writing in late 2019. I had not written before, outside of school or work, and summoned up the courage to publish an article on LinkedIn. It was as though a voice inside of me couldn't stay silent any longer. It didn't take long for me to learn how our stories impact others. Slowly but surely, people started to respond to my writing, and I felt a community begin to form as we engaged back and forth on each other's content. Each article over four months unleashed my voice further:

"People Matter - Lessons Learned from HR Tech, Boise & Chicago Startup Weeks"

"2020: Approaching a New Decade with Clarified Vision"

"18 years"

"A Built-In Seat at the Table"

An inkling of hope! Every time my voice was given a chance to sing out, community emerged as I readied myself to embark on planning for a new phase of life. And then on 12 March 2020, the world came crashing to a halt with the COVID pandemic, and my job did also. The whole world was impacted by the Corona virus, as we went into a global shutdown of business and life as we knew it. The death toll rose with no end in sight, and the oldest and most vulnerable were at the greatest risk.

Within forty-eight hours, this deep dip on my life map would explode into a new chapter and upward spiral of my own life. Our four adult children came home, and the six of us embraced this unexpected time together. My husband helped me start my Pieces of I website, and I taught myself how to build and create every page of it utilizing my own photography and writing. It was intriguing to watch my online community rally to help one another as we all endured the challenges of a closed-off, indoor world of uncertainty. While the world around us was scary, and we didn't know what would happen next, it was through community and compassionate care we would survive together. A new vision came through, and I wrote a new article, but this time, I published it from my own website in response to the craziness of the world around us:

> *Caring for Older Adults and Others At Risk During a Pandemic*
>
> *Quite simply, we can help those in need, and we must. Now is the time to evaluate our priorities and make changes to support those around us.*

At the same time, looking for a new job was difficult, as the rules of hiring were more challenging than ever. I was told to remove older experiences from my resume in order to appear younger. If I were to take those experiences off, my resume would neither reflect my capabilities nor represent what I had to offer in a new role. Decades would be diminished in an effort to avoid bias. The choice to leave my career was made in order to give my love, energy, and light to my family. This was a positive choice, not one to hide from, and it reflected the passion and commitment I bring to everything. Yes, I was older, but I wanted to be authentic and knew my blend of values, work experience, volunteering, and leadership roles in the community had its own place in the world. My 'why' came through strongly in alignment with my intentions: *To value each person for who they actually are.*

Searching for a job highlighted to me the importance of working with companies that had a culture of respect for every employee. I applied for many jobs where my resume was probably not even considered. It was humbling but aligned with my values and offered me the ability to dive deeper into creating this next phase of life more fully. When you finally reach the point of reclaiming your value and values, they become essential. My community continued to grow through my writing and networking with values-driven people and groups, and I found inspiration in their stories and willingness to help one another. In rapid succession, I began working with several people to expand our callings, both individually and collectively.

One of the first people I began working with was my friend Leslie who called to ask about my new website and to see how we could support one another. I had known Leslie for several years; we had volunteered together and were both passionate about empowering others. While listening to her story, it became evident we could have a tremendous impact by helping one another. Leslie was diagnosed with stage IV breast cancer two months after an all-clear mammogram and ultrasound; it was hidden in dense breast tissue, and she was determined to share her message about the implications of breast density: *So that her story does not become your story.*

Her mission was very specific in response to a challenge that impacts women worldwide (over 40% of women have dense breasts). While I do not have breast cancer, I do have dense breast tissue, and her story inspired me to learn and do more to help empower others. Together with a small team, we simplified and refined her mission to bring about what is now her nonprofit My Density Matters. We created and expanded the programs and partnerships to reach people in a new way, and I created the Empower Your Breast Health page of my website to help amplify the message. My online community came through with support for this cause, and the terms 'Mighty Warrior' and 'Mighty Warriors' were used to describe the many women who must battle for their own healthcare where inequities and challenges are prevalent. The people we met, and continue to meet, remind us we are better together on this mission to save lives through earlier detection.

A second calling, or awakening, came through a friend from LinkedIn who asked me to join a Friday night happy hour with entrepreneurs from around the country. The intention was to support one another through the many challenges of the pandemic, and while I didn't know anyone else on the call, I welcomed the growth opportunity. On the second happy hour call, however, I burst into tears and turned my camera off in response to a values exercise. We were supposed to discuss our relationship with a randomly assigned value, and I had gotten the word courage. It was a moment of reckoning for me, as I wanted to project positivity, but my relationship with this value had roots in the dips from my life map. Old painful moments of frustration, sadness, and loneliness were triggered, and I was neither prepared to respond nor reconcile with how to move forward. While the group on the call was kind, I was numb and stayed on to listen only. A few people reached out; it was humbling and made me cry harder, as I felt like a failure.

As courage would have it, I decided to return for a third call. The intention was for it to be my last, but I would show up, show everyone I was fine, and then never return. I felt the need to repair the damage I had done to my own ego. This time, however, one of the men on the call openly broke down in tears. He showed great courage. My heart felt strongly for his vulnerability and pain. In that moment, I was able to look in the mirror and see my real judge was me. The realization hit: *If I'm not accepted here for who I actually am, why would I want to return? But if I don't show up as who I am, am I really being accepted? What kind of belonging is there when I shame myself from even being who I really am?* It was time I brought my 'why' home to value myself for who I actually am.

I continued to return to this call and made new friends, colleagues, and business associates. Two small teams emerged: A team who brought the value culture to life and a team who helped learn about mental fitness together. These experiences helped transform me from the inside out. For the first time, I focused on myself. 'The good, the bad, and the ugly.' The learnings about judgment, saboteurs, and wisdom within each of us are built into the work I do and how I show up as a person.

Through it all, I unleashed my own inner artist. The combination of life experiences weaves throughout my writing and poetry, as I am now open to hearing and nurturing my voice and creativity. Along the way, I built a global community and have artists and value-based collaborative partners. They encourage me to continue to write, travel, take pictures, and share my voice as we collectively embrace our unique contributions to this world.

Now I see my own challenges and opportunities in a different way. I 'have had it all,' and I want to empower others to have it all too. It is our choice. We decide what all is, and then we can create pathways through learning to help us achieve our vision.

Within the four walls of every home and every company are layers of generational genius. My husband and four children continue to show me a whole new aspect of the world from their viewpoint. We share the 'teacher/mentor' baton as we teach one another about our changing world and combine ideas to create new solutions. I have learned whatever I needed to learn from whoever was willing to teach me—both young and old—in order to raise a family, consult, and build a business. The number-one lesson: We are better together; diversity makes us stronger. When you value each person for who they actually are, they will be your teammate, collaborator, and partner. You will succeed together.

To be successful, we need to be better at passing the baton back and forth between being a mentor and a mentee. Learning is endless; opportunities for growth are abundant. You can learn from each other at any age; therefore, life continues to be an exciting adventure. It is time to tell a new story about younger and older people coming together to solve problems—from the smallest to the biggest. There is no time like now to start. Let's do this together, shall we?

## About Susan LePlae Miller

Susan LePlae Miller is a social impact consultant, mental fitness coach, speaker, storyteller, and poet who helps you realize your vision by recognizing and releasing your potential. She partners with a global community to deliver compassionate care and values throughout her process of transformation.

Susan's website: www.piecesofi.com
Susan on LinkedIn: https://www.linkedin.com/in/susan-leplae-miller/
Pieces of I, LLC, on LinkedIn: https://www.linkedin.com/company/pieces-of-i-llc/
Facebook: https://www.facebook.com/piecesofi
Instagram: https://www.instagram.com/piecesofillc/
Twitter: https://twitter.com/PiecesofI
YouTube: https://www.youtube.com/@PiecesOfI

# CHAPTER 4

# When All Is Lost, There Is Hope Beyond Hope

Matthew Dickson

Have you ever wondered what you would do in a horrible situation like a tsunami or if you lost your legs or were trapped in rubble after an earthquake? How would you react? Do you wonder whether you would be strong enough to handle it?

I was faced with a horrible situation. I was blindsided. The pain and terror of what I was going through made me feel like I was being chased by a heat-seeking tornado. A relentless onslaught of death. This insidious beast chasing me was mental illness. A nice mix of schizophrenia, depression, and anxiety.

I grew up in St. Andrews, New Brunswick, Canada, a small seaside resort town. My mother was a nurse, and my father was a high school English teacher. I don't have many complaints about my youth. I was a straight-A student but could have had more confidence than I did. I liked playing golf, biking around the town, and going for runs. I did have an unmet need to go exploring, though. This came to a head in the middle of university when I decided to bicycle across Canada.

I was in my third year of engineering, but I wasn't enjoying it as much as I should have. My heart wasn't in it. Although I was fairly smart, I didn't have a clue what I wanted to do with my life. But throughout university, I didn't feel right. I had no idea what was going to come down the tubes for me at the end of university. When mental illness hit, it hit hard.

For five years of university, I struggled a bit with my thoughts and emotions. But I could still get good marks, feed myself, and live independently. I was on the university rowing team, did a triathlon, and even biked across Canada. But at the end of my studies, the tornado came for me. And I was put to the test.

If there's anything I would like to tell people after what I have been through, it is that you are capable of so much more than you think you are. I believe everybody has inside of themselves vast amounts of courage, determination, and resilience lying dormant, ready to be used at a moment's notice.

Navy SEALs are taught that they are capable of 20 times more than they think they are. The sheer effort it took me to withstand the pain coming from my body was tremendous. I was tormented. The anxiety was like a machete stuck through my chest. Just to sit still in a chair took a kind of will I didn't know was humanly possible.

If you do a search on the Internet for the phrase 'desperately trying to save their life,' countless headlines of news articles will show up. They will involve people drowning, being caught in natural disasters, being chased by wild animals, or other horrific situations.

People can understand why those people are desperate. They are trying to save their lives. They will use any means possible to do so. They are desperate. Desperate times call for desperate measures. So, when I found myself desperately trying to save *my* life, I wondered, *Why is it that people are sometimes scared to interact with you? Why do people walk past you?* These are questions with which I still wrestle. I have some ideas as to why we help some people who are desperate and not others, but some part of it still mystifies me.

———

I have read that when horrible things happen to you, the people in your life often leave you, unless you already have a deeper relationship with them. I know that this isn't set in stone. I heard about a man in the hospital; he was given no chance to live. One of his attendants came in and talked to him every day for months. Very few people came in to see him. He ended up making a full recovery, which essentially was a miracle. When asked what kept him going through it all, he responded that he did it for the hospital attendant. He said that he couldn't let him down and hung on because of him.

Miracles do happen. This is why I feel that it is important to build relationships with more depth in your life so that if disaster does strike in your life, there will be more people who know you and are more likely to stick with you. To get a deeper relationship with someone, start by simply sharing a bit more about yourself than you usually would. Get used to doing that with some of the people in your life. You'll find a little sharing can go a long way.

So, yes, I felt a sense of desperation that would take many years to go away. The experience of mental illness is also a very bewildering and confusing one. I always considered myself a nice guy. I have done some dumb things throughout my life, like everybody else, but overall, I thought I was a good person.

When mental illness struck me and started altering my thoughts and emotions, it was very confusing for me. Also, I didn't understand what schizophrenia was (this was 1994, before mental illness was even talked about in mainstream conversation). What was schizophrenia? I didn't know what it was or did to a person.

So, I wondered, *Am I evil? Does this mean that I will do bad things?* And that terrified me. And this was on top of the terror I already felt with the disease. I never had any thoughts about wanting to hurt anyone, but the confused part of my brain couldn't make sense of this. I went for about six to eight years living this way until I read a sentence somewhere that said, "People with schizophrenia are no more violent than the rest of the general population." I breathed a sigh of relief. I was so glad that this meant I wasn't evil and wasn't going to hurt anyone. But at the same time, I thought, *Why didn't anyone tell me this at the very beginning when I was first diagnosed?*

They say knowing is half the battle. I fully agree. Sometimes I think knowing might be more than half, even 90% at times. With mental illness, you can also feel very helpless and defenseless. I felt like the people around me felt helpless as well because there wasn't anything they could do to relieve me of my pain. I felt like everyone was looking at me, wondering whether I was okay, not knowing what to do in a lot of situations. It was a miserable experience for everyone involved—but there is hope, and more hope than you even realize.

People who survived jumping off the Golden Gate Bridge in San Francisco were asked what they thought the moment after they jumped, when there was no turning back. Many of them instantly regretted it. One moment, they were all for jumping; the next, they wished they hadn't. I wish more people knew this fact about those who had jumped. It goes to show that, yes, you can hold on for longer than you thought. Even when you have no hope, there is still hope. There is *hope beyond hope.*

At the end of my fifth year of engineering, I went to get help. I went to the university health clinic. They took me to the local hospital, and thus, I entered the mental health system. The doctors found a medication that worked. I stayed on it. I never went off it. It worked, but it worked painfully slowly, or what I like to call 'glacially' slowly.

One percent of the population worldwide gets schizophrenia. I never hallucinated, but 75% of people with schizophrenia do hallucinate, and the hallucinations can be any of the five senses. Also, some hallucinations can be very beautiful and enjoyable. Many, though, are relentlessly tormenting.

I had psychotic symptoms, but not hallucinations. My body felt very fragile. Some people with schizophrenia feel like their body will go down the drain when they shower. I didn't feel that way, but I could understand what that might feel like for people.

Some people think the person on TV is talking to them. I knew that wasn't true, but people on TV did feel alarmingly 'in the room with me.' I was never classified as 'paranoid.' I never thought the CIA was spying on me through the phone or TV like some people with schizophrenia do. I had to take a tranquilizer once after watching an action movie in the theatre because it felt like the action in the movie was actually happening in the theatre, although I knew it wasn't.

In my worst year, someone saw me walking down the street, and they said I looked like I was "walking through a world of flying glass." I thought that was very accurate and described my experience perfectly. Like every step could be my last. It felt like bullets were being fired, and bombs were being thrown at me, although I knew they weren't, and it was a nice day, and I was just going for a stroll through town on a lovely day.

There is still mystery around the disease. There can be a hereditary component. It can sometimes skip generations, a grandparent giving it to a grandchild. There could be environmental components to it. Schizophrenia is not a split personality, although split and multiple personality disorders do exist.

I've read that mental illness can be prevented. If I had lived a healthier lifestyle, I don't know whether that could have prevented me from getting schizophrenia. However, there are factors that can help or hinder you. If you have too many hindrances, that could lower your chances for recovery.

Disorganized thinking is a symptom of schizophrenia. My thoughts were like taking a book, mixing up every single word in the book, and getting me to read it—with every single word out of order. But even though my thoughts were racing and jumbled, part of my thoughts was working just fine.

Other people with schizophrenia say this too. I could still have thoughts like "What should I have for breakfast today? Hmmm, I think I feel like eggs." Or "Maybe I could go for a walk this afternoon at 2 p.m." Or bigger thoughts like "I think I'll go back to school and finish my degree."

Another way to describe my thoughts is that I could think about things specifically but not generally. It was hard to put things into categories or use comparisons or parallels, hence the disorganization of thoughts. This also made it hard to use humor. I had always enjoyed making people laugh in my youth. I sorely missed this for many years, as I tried to make jokes, but they just didn't work. That made me very sad.

When a psychiatrist walked up to me in the psychiatric ward one day and said "We've been discussing what your diagnosis is, Matthew, and we think you have schizophrenia. Hopefully, with some treatment, we can get you better again," that was a real bomb to drop. *Schizophrenia? I've got what?*

After I absorbed that, I approached a nurse in the ward and asked how long it might take to get better. She said, "Sometimes it takes a couple of years before you feel like yourself again." I don't know where she got that two-year time frame, but that was all I had to go on.

After that, I asked myself, "Do I fight this, or do I end my life?" For five to 10 seconds, my mind went blank. Then, out of nowhere, I thought, *I'm going to fight this.* I don't know where that thought came from, but I am very thankful for it.

My next thought was, *Okay, now that you've decided to fight this, how are you going to do it?* My mind went blank for another five to 10 seconds. Then, again, out of nowhere, I thought, *I'm going to put my life on hold. I accept the fact that I will do nothing I enjoy for two years (as per what the nurse had told me). If, when two years come up, I am back to normal, I will pick my life up from where I left off and move on with my life.*

My next thought was, *Okay, now that you've got a plan, when are you going to start this?* Then I could really feel time ticking, like I couldn't wait on this plan for too long. So, I thought, *Maybe there's a show on in the TV room (of the psych ward). I think I'll go in and watch a show.*

So, I got up out of my chair and started walking across the floor to the TV room. It was a very purposeful stride. It felt like I was 'running the gauntlet,' head down, walking straight into the oncoming fire, instead of running the other way. It was an act of bravery and courage, trying to do the right thing against seemingly insurmountable odds. Note the word 'seemingly.'

The actress Carrie Fisher had bipolar and said people with mental illness should be awarded medals of bravery for what they do every day. I and millions of people worldwide should have entire rooms of our homes filled with these medals. Maybe one day I'll get a medal.

Note 'seemingly.' It seems impossible, but it isn't. Being asked to defy gravity is impossible, and that's what it felt like I was being asked to do. But you can last a lot longer than you think. You can do so much more than you think, like Navy SEALs are taught in their training. But I didn't know that starting out.

Time went by slowly. Every day seemed the same. Yet everything was so chaotic. The outside of my life was pretty peaceful. I didn't have a lot of problems in my life other than mental illness and minor other hindrances, but the disease made me feel like my life was a whirlwind.

Every day felt the same, and everything was chaotic at the same time. It is an odd juxtaposition. I don't know how chaos can feel so unbelievably boring, but that's the way it felt—unpredictable and monotonous. And my medication kept working. I noticed a small improvement each week throughout my whole recovery.

I never had any problems with substance abuse. I was in and out of the psych ward at the hospital five or six times in 1994. I lived in a group home from 1995 to 1997. Then I got an apartment, which was scary for me, but I did it anyway. I got a job doing data entry and filing in an office. I would be there for the next 21 years.

I always tried to push myself. I had to pace myself by trying to do more and trying new things, yet not taking on too much that would make me regress. In 2000, I bought my first car. In 2005, I bought my first house. In 2015, I made a fitness website.

In 2000, I started educating myself more on how to get better. I read books on mental health, diet and exercise, people skills, and finances. I have learned so much from all the books I've read and all the Internet searches I've done. They have made my life so much easier. That is one thing I highly encourage more people to do: to start dabbling in the personal development field. Personal development is used by Olympic athletes, world leaders, elite soldiers, businesspeople, and everyday people like me.

I also developed more empathy for people struggling with things. And for people in general. More empathy, compassion, respect, and kindness. I always knew how hard life could be, but after going through mental illness, I developed a newfound knowledge of the difficulties and complexities of life.

In 2017, I heard for the first time about mental health in developing countries. I had never thought about that before. If people have no clean water, no schools, and malaria, what do they do if they have depression, anxiety, or bipolar? It is a concept so simple, but I had never thought about it before. It had never been spelled out for me.

I went through mental illness in one of the best countries to do so. Yet it felt like I was living in a war zone. My heart goes out to people in impoverished or war-torn countries who have mental illness and the atrocities of poverty and war to go through as well. So, in 2018, I launched my Mind Aid website to try to help them. I believe if everybody simply knew about mental health in developing countries, if it became a mainstream conversation, millions of people would want to help.

I am finding peace and contentment in my life again. I didn't know if I would ever again see that, but with tremendous effort on my part and an equal amount of pure luck, I have. Now, I get to think, ponder, and reflect on things, large and small. I really enjoy listening to the wind rustling the leaves in the trees. I get to see sunsets and actually enjoy looking at them

... instead of it being painful and incredibly boring. I get to look at the stars in the sky at night and wonder about what's out there instead of what felt like looking at a very mundane image of salt sprinkled on black paper.

I get control over my body. I get to dream and do things I want to do, things that are enjoyable, not painful things I'm forced to do against my will. I get to sit in silence. I get to listen to that still, small voice in my head—a voice of reassurance, comfort, dreams, and desires. I get to feel confident, knowing I've walked through 'flying glass.' Daily life has become easier for me—not perfect but easier. I've grown and become stronger—not invincible but more solid.

I get to laugh and tell jokes. I get a second chance. Not everyone gets that. I can't sit here and keep the knowledge I have of getting through a maze-like hell and not share it with others going through that same maze. I want to reach out to them in the maze as they sit terrified in the dark, in the agony, alone, unheard, unseen, and show them a way out. Give them a map of the maze and point to the way out! Show them where the light at the end of the tunnel is because that light exists. People need to know where that light is.

People need hope—desperately. I can't sit here and not give it to them. It is my duty to show them the way. That's the funny thing about life. No one is demanding me to do this. The government isn't demanding I help other people with mental illness. When you think about it, the situation is so dire for so many people; maybe it should be demanded of me! In either case, my conscience demands it of me.

My dream is to have Mind Aid be a conversation starter for people everywhere to bring awareness to mental health in developing countries. What some people have to go through is unthinkable. If mental health in developing countries could become as well-known as clean water or mosquito bed nets, think of the help they could get.

So, what would you do if you saw the tsunami wave coming up the shore toward you? What would you do if you were trapped in your car as it sunk below the surface of a rushing river? That untapped potential lying dormant your whole life would immediately kick into action. You would do what you didn't think was humanly possible. And when you don't think you have any more left to give, when it seems there is just no hope left, please remember: *There is Hope Beyond Hope.*

## About Matthew Dickson

Matthew Dickson helps people with mental illness in developing countries so they can get access to basic mental health care through his Mind Aid platform.

Mind Aid acts as a hub that steers people toward organizations working for the cause. These organizations use models of basic mental health care that are low-cost, proven effective, and scalable.

Some of these organizations have been endorsed by Bill Clinton, Forest Whitaker, Arcade Fire, Ashley Judd, Zak Williams (son of Robin Williams), and Tim Shriver (founder of the Special Olympics).

Matthew has successfully recovered from schizophrenia and has bicycled across Canada.

CHAPTER 5

# Just When You Thought You Couldn't

—

## Dr. Jo Anne White

No one would go near her. The open sores covering her arms from the constant biting of herself were visible and raw. They looked as if they were never given a chance to heal. If they weren't off-putting enough, the unpleasant scent of urine that surrounded her daily was, but she couldn't help herself. Thin with wiry arms and legs and unfocused light brown eyes that looked everywhere, yet nowhere. Her dark brown hair seemed to continually cover her face as though she wanted to be hidden. Maybe it was safer for Maria to remain covered and concealed to go unnoticed. I could only surmise but without any real certainty.

She made wordless sounds, noises like squeaks and squeals, except when upset. At that time, the sound was low and guttural. I was her camp counselor. Maria was in my care, along with five other children who had challenges speaking, communicating, and interacting. Yet she was the one who bewildered me the most. It seemed that many people had already given up on her, deeming her hopeless and helpless.

In my mind and my heart, I was determined to find a way; although I didn't know what that would be or even look like. I was going on instinct and compassion, which was an innate part of me. How could we turn our backs, our support, and our attention away from someone who needed help? To me, that was a daunting and disturbing mystery. I had just turned eighteen and would be starting college in the fall, majoring in English Literature, which I loved. My dreams of being a successful writer were ignited years before in my early childhood. They grew stronger as I began to shape my future and my career.

The only group of children labeled special needs amid a bustling day camp of many kids of different ages and their counselors was mine. We were already deemed the untouchables. Since I was in charge of them, I, too, was included in the pariah category. It wasn't unusual for me to stand out and be different. I had come up against that earlier in my life. My way of learning was atypical. It caused me much upset and self-doubt in the past. I had to painfully heal from that for some time by releasing the opinions of teachers and others that, unfortunately, I had adopted as my own. Releasing and letting go of the belief that I wasn't good enough and would never amount to anything wasn't easy. Yet it was a powerful journey of healing and growing stronger within me on the road of my ongoing self-discovery.

My manner of being, which was also different from the so-called norm, was cultivated by me and distinctly my own. Some scars still remained from my younger years. I hadn't conquered everything. Yet I had overcome so much and was gaining more confidence in myself. That's probably why I felt such empathy for the children I was in charge of, who didn't fit in and who were kept distant and apart from others. Having directly experienced what it was like and devising ways to get past it and surmount it, I believed, made me a good fit to work with these children. I had to find and create ways to personally cope with all of it—from not fitting in to working with my own neural differences and negative self-beliefs to function and ultimately conquer. If I could do that for myself, wasn't it possible—no, essential and responsible—to help others? The answer, to me, was obvious.

I didn't have everything figured out about life, about myself, or the road ahead by any means. That continuous discovery or uncovering takes time—maybe even a lifetime. There were moments of self-doubt that would creep in that I had to contend with. Yet it felt as if my journey was unfolding even in ways I hadn't foreseen. My determination to work with these children in my care was strong, but I wasn't totally sure of myself at this time. I felt clueless as to what to do with the children, especially with Maria. My crew was eyed strangely by the other children at camp. They kept a large safe distance between us so interaction, if there was any, was minimal to non-existent. However, the feelings, sometimes even outright hostility or disparaging remarks, were strongly transmitted. I knew I had to do something to change the situation, especially with Maria who appeared to be the child most reviled even by her own group and by other counselors who should have known better.

Maria was self-abusive. It's a strong word to describe her behavior, but she was hurting herself daily. Maria seemed oblivious to the disdain that others had for her. She conveniently lived in her own world of internal sounds while hurting herself at every turn. The unknown was whether it would lessen or stop by itself, which didn't seem to be the case thus far. The bigger question that I wrestled with was, would it shift with some intervention? If so, what kind and how?

The behavior my children exhibited was very new to me, and I was processing it all. This much I knew: even though I wanted to work with these children, I was still figuring it out. One of my gifts, which I'm very grateful for, is my intuitive abilities. Today, in addition to my coaching, counseling, and training, I also teach others how to open and connect to their intuition and the many facets of their inner guidance. I believe that my intuition served me even then.

Instinctively, I began singing with Maria whenever we had the opportunity to be alone or even together with the group. The other children responded, and even attempted to sing at times, but not Maria. At first, she ignored me as if I wasn't even there or I was somehow invisible. It took patience and some time, days and days, in fact, until she acknowledged me and my singing. One day, as I sang, Maria turned in my direction, not looking at me, just staring outward. It was a small sign, but a sign nevertheless, which, to me, was encouraging. Deciding I wouldn't give up, I kept at it, and soon, something more happened.

Although I was the only one singing and humming, Maria seemed to respond to the rhythm and my voice. Another milestone was taking place. I sang some more, and she opened her mouth but didn't sing or utter a sound. It was then that I noticed that her arms were not the only body part of her that was scarred with open self-inflicted wounds. She was also biting the inside of her mouth. Her gums looked red, irritated, and swollen. How painful was it to drink, swallow, or even open her mouth after so much biting of the flesh, I wondered. I could only imagine the pain she was enduring, or was she numb to that too? I began to ever so gently massage her cheeks from the outside in the hopes of getting her to stop hurting herself. At first, she pulled away.

Yet over time, Maria began to trust me a bit more, so I tried again. This time, she didn't draw back from me. Maria seemed to respond to my light kneading of her cheeks: another form of stimulation, different from her own, that wasn't hazardous or hurtful. In fact, it may have been soothing to her, although I wasn't certain. This seemed to calm her somewhat. Yet it didn't bring anyone closer to her or get anyone wanting to connect with her. She appeared not to mind their distance. Although it was hard to ascertain since Maria couldn't or wouldn't communicate. One of the biggest hurdles that kept people at a safe distance, unfortunately, was the unmistakable urine odor. How would I handle that? Was it even possible?

We had time during the day for swimming in the pool, which my group liked, although they weren't great swimmers, if at all. However, being in cooling water on a hot summer day was a real treat and one they didn't want to pass up. They splashed around in shallow water that was under-knee deep with shrieks of pleasure, excitement, and sometimes fear. Maria never entered the pool. Instead, she just sat on the edge, dangling her feet and biting the skin on her arm. It gave me an idea. Just because she didn't like swimming in the pool, that didn't mean that she was opposed to getting wet. A plan was brewing in my mind that I mulled over later that evening when I was home with my mother in the apartment. In the morning, as I was readying for work, I wondered just how I would pull off my new plan of action.

We were getting ready for our swimming activity. As luck or divine intervention would have it, I had some additional help that day, which was rare. I decided to take advantage of the extra set of hands, ears, and eyes and implement my idea. The children were putting on their bathing suits with help from both me and Carole, the assistant, but Maria was on the bench, staring into space.

"Maria," I called to her, and she shook her head as if listening without turning to look. I walked over to where she was on the bench, with her feet swinging back and forth in agitated or restless motion. "Let's get your bathing suit on," I suggested. She hardly ever put the suit on, although it came with her daily. My words seemed to increase her uneasiness. "I promise that you won't have to swim or even get into the pool. I have a better idea," I spoke gently, yet firmly.

I was already suited up. Somehow, she believed my words and let me help her get out of her clothes and into the yellow and green bathing suit. I began singing, and this time, Maria smiled. I grabbed Maria's hand and swung it playfully back and forth while singing and walking, even prancing with her to the shower. Carole had already been alerted to what I was going to do. She and I exchanged nods and eye contact as I walked further away and down the hallway.

Still holding Maria's hand, I leaned into the shower and adjusted the knobs so the temperature was not too hot or cold. When it seemed the right temperature, I gently coaxed her to move forward while I danced playfully. Maria and I entered the shower stall. I sang while I helped her wash her arms and legs. She didn't want to get her face or head wet, but she was letting me show her how to wash herself. It seemed that she wasn't only cooperating; Maria appeared to be enjoying the full experience.

This was the beginning of a stronger connection between us and became a consistent ritual whenever possible. One of the other bonuses which I had truly aimed for and desired was achieved. The urine odor had drastically diminished through the consistent showering. Now the other children in our group ventured closer to her without turning up their noses, frowning, or uttering insults. Maria was also relating more favorably to me. When I sang and swayed back and forth, she joined me without hesitation. No words were uttered, but big smiles covered her face. She would rock back and forth against my shoulder somewhat erratically, moving jerkily in time to the music. This was a major victory, and I was elated.

As the summer drew on, Maria seemed to come out of her shell even more. The sores on her arms weren't as red and swollen as before. She seemed to be biting herself less, which was a wonderful sign. Perhaps feeling more connected, supported, and included made all the difference in Maria not mutilating herself. She still didn't really talk, yet she was blossoming in other ways. Maria joined us more in the group activities rather than remaining isolated and aloof. The other children smiled with her, and she finally became a true member of our group, participating more than ever before. Not only was Maria changing, but also, working with her and with the other children had begun to change me too.

Being able to successfully help Maria with what was considered unconventional methods at the time gave me more than just hope. It excited me and expanded my compassion and vision while shifting my goals and creating new horizons in my mind that I never imagined. I now wanted to help and serve children with special needs and give them and their families more than hope. To have the ability to touch someone, help them change, learn and grow—through acceptance, genuine caring, and humanizing and connecting approaches—was a gift to me as well. I believe that we're here for many reasons. One of those reasons is to serve in whatever capacity, any large or small way, that we can.

When contemplating the writing of this chapter, I thought about focusing on the many personal challenges that I've come through and mostly overcome. Yet what was stirring in me was to share another person's struggles that sadly caused them to unfavorably stand out. Their differences and other people's biases and judgments, unfortunately, kept them apart and separate from others and the mainstream of society and from all it had to offer.

My working with children didn't stop as a camp counselor. I shifted my undergraduate degree, and instead of English Literature, I majored in education and special education. Despite some undeniable learning challenges that still presented themselves throughout the educational process, I earned my master's and Ph.D. I went on to teach children with special needs and neuro differences and even became an executive director of a comprehensive educational, clinical, vocational, and residential program serving children and youth with special needs. I eventually became the director of research, evaluation, and training for the entire Bancroft family of programs. Later on, I earned multiple certifications and expanded my way of serving others by becoming a coach and counselor. I had to heal various injuries and found and studied alternative modalities and forms of healing to restore myself to better health and improved functioning and to later utilize and incorporate them in my work with other people.

I write this not to toot my own horn but to emphasize to you that anything can be possible with perseverance, self-belief, and drive. I didn't always believe in myself or my capabilities. We don't have to be stuck in outdated beliefs or messages that really may not be true about ourselves. We have the ability to change those beliefs and transform ourselves in the process.

I will never give up writing since it is, has been, and will be an integral part of me. However, the call to help others to somehow guide them through the hard times to find strength, support, confidence, and effective approaches is powerful, deep, and forever growing in me. Both call up my passion, energy, and life purpose.

Many of us have areas in which we excel and feel comfortable. We may even exceed our own expectations and the expectations of others. However, we can also have realms in which we feel challenged or have difficulty whereby we just can't seem to get a handle on things. It's not always easy to live in a fast-paced and ever-changing world with so much to tackle, understand, and learn. We can get overwhelmed, even anxious, especially if we don't seem to follow the projected way of being in the world. We may perform differently, learn or behave differently, which can make us appear dissimilar, strange, and even weird to others. It can seem that way to us as well. If we have what others may call or consider deficits or disabilities, that can also hinder us in countless ways.

There are many famous people who've had and have challenges of various kinds—some they could overcome, some they had to adapt to, and some whose challenge became their greatest strength. In all of these individuals, what stands out the most to me and is paramount for all of us to know and embrace is that no matter the difficulty, they never gave up. They continued to find ways and answers to help themselves learn, grow, and thrive. That's a powerful message to absorb.

Do you have a disability or medical condition? You're not alone, and it's nothing to be ashamed of or to hide from. People with disabilities include actors, actresses, celebrities, singers, world leaders, scientists, presidents, inventors, and many other famous people. There are also millions of people in the world who aren't famous or well-known who live with, battle, and overcome their disabilities daily.

Thomas Edison was deemed a difficult and hyperactive student. Despite his erratic academic learning, his achievements were vast. He developed effective ways to learn and study on his own, which helped him make and shape history. Edison invented the phonograph, the motion picture camera, and the light bulb. Walt Disney had learning challenges, but despite them, he became an animator, cartoonist, and the creator of Disneyland.

Are you often beset by self-doubts, self-condemnation, or feeling of unworthiness as I was? That way of thinking, those habitual messages in your brain, whether from life circumstances or other people's perceptions, can be changed. It's a worthwhile process to come to a place of peace within you for yourself. Know that it is achievable. You have to want it and go after it. When you do, you can come to experience more ease and confidence in yourself.

Do you feel as though you don't fit in and wonder if there's something wrong with you because of it? Fitting in may not be all it's depicted to be. By not following the popular way of being or by having different interests and motivations as I did may accentuate your uniqueness. It can help you blaze and follow your own path that others want to trail behind.

My mind no longer rages at me with belittling comments. Today, it's not unusual to hear inside my head "You got this." Yes, it took time and self-work, but it was so worth it. I learned by working with myself and others that it's important to celebrate the steps we take, even the small ones, as we move forward toward our own greatness. It takes time. Being our own cheerleader rather than our worst critic can aid us in acquiring the confidence we need. With it, we gain momentum to follow through, persist, and advance. Find power and inspiration within yourself. It's there, waiting to be uncovered or discovered by you.

If you need to get assistance, reach out for the help you need. We often think it's just our problem, and no one else ever experiences or undergoes this. Or that we have to figure it totally out for ourselves. That's not the case. You don't have to do it all alone. Getting the help and support you need is not a weakness but a sign of strength and self-compassion.

No matter the differences and unique abilities/disabilities that you have, don't let anything stand in your way of following your heart, your dreams, passions, and what excites you. Whether challenges, setbacks, or temporary defeats are present, stand up for yourself and don't despair. Remind yourself that they don't and won't define you. Believe in yourself above all else. Self-belief is powerful and opens doors, new perceptions, and a willingness to tackle what's in your path and move forward to create and live out an amazing destiny that is uniquely yours and distinctively you.

Remind yourself as my mind now advises me that you can do this. Be determined that you can overcome whatever is in your path so that you can undoubtedly be and become the most amazing you that you are born and meant to be!

# About Dr. Jo Anne White

Dr. Jo Anne White is an international #1 bestselling, award-winning author, speaker, and consultant. She's recognized as a Goodwill Global Ambassador for civil and humanitarian work in education, entrepreneurship, coaching, and women's issues. Dr. White was also named a Worldwide Branding Top Female Executive in Professional Coaching by Worldwide Who's Who. As a certified life, spiritual, and business coach, counselor and energy master teacher, she empowers and inspires men, women, families, and businesses to achieve greater health and wellness, master success, realize their dreams, thrive, and triumph. She's also the executive producer and host of the *Power Your Life* shows.

Early in her career, she taught children with special needs and was an adjunct instructor in the Special Education Department at Temple University. Dr. White was hired as the executive director of a comprehensive educational, clinical, vocational, autistic, residential, and community program for children and youth with special needs at Bancroft in New Jersey. She later served as their director of research, evaluation, and training for all Bancroft programs.

Known as the 'Success Doc' to global audiences, Doc White gets to the heart of what matters most to businesses, organizations, and people with her transformative and inspiring seminars, coaching programs, and products. She has designed and delivered imaginative training programs, seminars, and curriculum for universities, churches, non-profit organizations, medical facilities, corporations, and companies such as *Temple*

*University, GlaxoSmithKline, West Jersey Hospital,* and *Women in Communications.*

As the CEO of Dr. Jo Anne White Consulting Services, LLC, she teaches people how to overcome adversity and turn challenges into opportunities while helping businesses and organizations build unified teams and create more personal and professional success. Doc White has been featured online, in national and international publications such as CNN.com, Good Housekeeping, and WebMD. She made frequent guest appearances on radio and television networks such as NBC, CBS, CN8, FOX, World Talk Radio, and Voice of America sharing her expertise.

Website: www.drjoannewhite.com
Email: joanne@drjoannewhite.com
FB: www.facebook.com/joanne.white.543
FB Business Page: www.facebook.com/Dr.JoAnneWhite/
LinkedIn: www.linkedin.com/in/joannewhite
Twitter: https://twitter.com/JWPowerYourLife
Instagram: www.instagram.com/jwpoweryourlife/
YouTube: www.youtube.com/user/docWhite2
Power Your Life Radio Show: www.blogtalkradio.com/jo-anne-white

CHAPTER 6

# From the Darkest Day to Blackest Night Transforming to Light and Love

———

Brad Burchnell

### *The Path Not of My Choosing*

It was the night of November 30, 2020, and I had just received notification at the end of my shift at work that I would be given two months off to address my 'issues.' Since my daughter had taken her life on May 30, 2018, my emotional, mental, and physical state had taken a major hit. I was empty, and the divorce (my second one) just made me feel even more worthless with each passing moment that I could hardly breathe or, for that matter, continue breathing. FMLA? People would see that I was gone, and they would talk about me! How could I ever face going back? Let alone showing my face outside of my house. I was truly dangling at the end of my rope with no knot at the end to hold onto and an abyss below.

I had experienced suicidal ideations a great deal over my life since being bullied in my ninth-grade year. I never felt good enough, wanted, or of any value to myself, let alone anyone else. I faced my mortality and wondered, *Can I pull the trigger? Can I?* I made sure that it was unloaded and then pulled the trigger. It was as if a lightning bolt coursed through my veins. I immediately locked it away and booked a flight out to California to stay with my mom and brother until after the first day of the year.

Holy crap! What a way to start a chapter off with Brad! Well, this is my path and my journey from the state of despair, where I felt shame, guilt (survivors' guilt), and faced the diagnosis of PTSD. PTSD, me? I had never seen combat in any of the 15 years that I served in the Navy, not even when I was serving during Desert Storm. So, it left me wondering, *Where did it all come from?* It was unrecognized and unhealed issues from my childhood. It was also compounded during my daughter's downward spiral that began in 2007. Her first attempt in 2016 left me fearful and having to prepare for the potential and likelihood that she would be successful as I had read in several psychological journals and studies. My worst fear culminated with her ending her life in 2018. Unresolved childhood, adolescent, and adult trauma that had never been addressed was in a word: 'overwhelming.' It was my breaking point and the beginning of the healing that I desperately needed.

### Transformative Healing

The car arrived very early to take me to the airport, and my driver was very kind. The banter and discussion was light all the while the darkness and tumult were raging within. What was I feeling? I was feeling depressed, highly anxious, and nervous; filled with guilt and shame. Of these emotions, the one that is the most detrimental is shame. Shame has been defined by one of my favorite authors and speakers, Brene Brown, Ph.D., as an "intensely painful feeling or experience of believing that we are flawed and therefore unworthy of love and belonging" (Suttie, 2017)[1]. It was not that I was feeling bad; it was feeling that I *was* bad. Bad as someone that couldn't protect his daughter from herself; bad as a father that was estranged from his other daughters due to poor decisions that

---

1        (Suttie, 2017)

resulted in divorce. The inner critic and self-limiting belief that I was a bad person was the overriding narrative that was ruminating within my mind. It was exactly how I was feeling.

Though I had not yet begun the true deep work that I would begin in a few months, it was at the heart of how I was feeling and what was shaping my inner turmoil and desperation. To be honest, I didn't know what to expect when I arrived at my mom's home in California. I flew home in a kind of fog. I recognized people, places, the airport, the aircraft, others onboard, and the directions of the flight crew. I couldn't tell you very much about the conversations that I had that day. I stopped over in Dallas, where I made my way to the bar; food and alcohol would fix everything, I thought. It numbed but gave nothing back. I climbed onboard my final leg home and fell asleep on the plane. The next thing I recall was the words of the flight crew and their instructions to prepare for landing.

During the coming days leading up to Christmas, I spent the time visiting with my mom, my brother, and a good friend of mine from high school. I never spoke of the reason for my coming other than that I needed to be away from Michigan and be with family. The days came and went as did alcohol after my brother had gone to bed. Numbing seemed to be my strategy of choice and not a very good one. The sleep with the accompanied nightmares of my daughter just out of my reach … as she stepped off the apartment building, just beyond my grasp, and my other daughters pointing fingers at me. Looking at me, they began asking me with tears in their eyes, "Why wasn't it you instead of sissy?" That became a recurring nightmare that I could not shake and made me more fearful of sleeping.

The men's group I had joined—The Uncivilized Nation, founded by Traver Boehm, with the focus of helping men find their purpose and acknowledge their pain—I thought would be a place to start. Central to the group was a focus and practice on transforming and healing. There were group calls, local meetings, and other online events with various guest speakers. One event that forever changed my life and led me back to a place of healing occurred on December 20, 2020. It was a breathwork session with Leila Dylla. Leila is a life coach, yoga teacher, meditation guide, energy healer, and divine worker of breath. She led a dynamic breathwork session that required you to be on your back. I thought to myself, *That's odd but OK*. I can only describe the session as tantric. We were led to experience and allow our bodies just be. Whatever we were feeling, we were directed to allow it to unfurl before us like clouds and know that whatever happened, we were safe. Then, as she ramped us up into the meat of the session, she directed each of us to feel that hidden trauma that we never had acknowledged.

Issues with my mom and dad as a child, adolescent bullying, divorce, and all stemming from lack of self-trust all flooded me within. It was in a word, 'overwhelming.' Here I was, a mature male that had served in the military, and I was laying there, stunned, with uncontrollable tears rolling down the sides of my face. I finally could name what I was feeling. I was feeling a lack of safety and trust within me, and it came from unhealed parts of my inner child. It was a breakthrough and one that I really needed in order to move forward. Leila is a 'badass' (there's no other word to describe her), as I, lying on my back, could hear her voice bringing us back to center, all the while feeling my head buzzing, with my body electrified. The letters PTSD kept forming in my mind over and over again. What's the next step?

### The Healing Journey Through BREATH Framework ™

The next few weeks were somewhat chaotic, but I started to sleep somewhat better, and the nightmares began to abate. When I returned home, it was just after New Year's, and the house was empty, as I lived alone. I began coaching sessions with two amazing souls, Annie Leib and Michael Padurano. I had talked to them about going into coaching and finished up therapy with my therapist. As we began to meet regularly, they offered to meet with me at the same time, as their clients seemed to do better with the dynamic of two. They began to tag-team me about being on an inaugural program that they called the BREATH Framework™. My mentality was, *Sure, I can do that.* I was also thinking, *I can teach them a few things at the same time.*

Here's what I discovered: each step of the BREATH built upon each other. '**B**' for the beginning and knowing where you are starting from; understanding what 'you think you know' about yourself, your self-limiting beliefs, and traumas. OK, not really fun, but over a month of four sessions and a group call, there was a great amount of discovery of internal narrative that you don't recognize readily about yourself, but it comes into focus. Through this discovery, you understand where you have given away your 'power'; some might call it control. The '**R**' for 'reclaim your power' aided me in better understanding who and what *I* had given control over to and how it overshadowed who *I* was, who *I* wanted to be, and how *I* operated. These subtle power drains over time robbed me of self-trust, self-worth, self-validation, self-love, and self-acceptance that enables each of us to truly be whole.

The '**E**' component of excavating one's core values was a pure revelation to me, as I had no real understanding of what they entailed, but they were central to developing boundaries with people and circumstances. I looked at a word bank inventory of 250 core value words and initially chose over 20 and reduced them to the core values that I have today that define who I am and what I want to know myself as. They are:

1. Presence – when I am with someone or doing a task, I am with that person or task because quality time, for me, speaks as a language of love greater than mere words ever can.

2. Courage – doing hard things in spite of what might happen. Having difficult conversations and not just fun ones. Not shrinking away, and not operating from ego; being present and holding firm to my boundaries.

3. Integrity – something that I had not practiced a great deal in the past and one I knew was required. To be transparent, honest, and vulnerable and behave in a manner that was trustworthy not only to others but most importantly to myself.

4.  Empathy – relating to others with a shared knowledge of understanding and drawing from my experiences in my life's journey when relating to others on all occasions.

Little did I know it at the time, but this would be an important component of my life's work and passion in not only helping others but also in a corporate setting as well. It shaped my thought process and ability to address discomfort with ease and calm.

'**A**' was the worst part, as it represents 'allow.' Allowing myself the time to address the numerous traumas, pain, hurts, discomforts, failures, disappoints, and everything in-between, then laying them all down and moving away from them. It also provided me with a means to recognize triggering moments while getting curious about the emotions and feelings that I was experiencing. I was experiencing understanding about my 'why' and 'what' moments. This was a dynamic shift from within. It was true freedom and realization that not only could I be freed from my past mistakes, but also, I wasn't my past mistakes. They did not define me but rather refined me. I also realized that not only was I not perfect, but also, I didn't have to be either. I realized that after reading Brene Brown's book, *The Gifts of Imperfection*. It was a game-changer for me.

Going through '**T**' was the next step in my journey, and it was no different than the previous steps, but I was now in a greater state of peace and understanding of who I was and what was ahead. I no longer felt that I needed to stay in a moment-by-moment construct during my day. I could now begin to look at the future with expectation, rather than dread. Imagine you are looking from one side of the putrid swamp, and you are hip-deep in a foul-smelling, hot environment, and bugs are surrounding you. Not a great picture, is it? Well, that was exactly where I was. I was beginning to come out of that swamp and realize that this work was coming to an end in the next month; however, I felt more inspired and ready for the next steps.

Now we arrive at the last step, '**H**.' Healing is a daily activity that is ongoing. It requires mindfulness, resilience, patience, gratitude, joy, self-love, self-trust, self-care, critical self-awareness, and self-reflection every day. It doesn't mean that we are complete by any means; at least it doesn't for me. It does mean that we are better equipped to address the issues that had kept us (well, me anyway) in a place that I could not see a way forward previously.

I started the process with Mike and Annie with an attitude of *I'll show them* because I thought that I knew better than they did. After all, I had more experience in life than they had, didn't I? I found out that these two people would arrive at a place in my life that would leave an indelible mark within that I can never repay other than paying it forward and providing to others. I read recently that someone said, "Giving back means taking something in the first place." That was a learning moment for me as well, and one that I now choose to tell others—that I provide to others and not give back. It is my hope that this portion and chapter provides others **hope**.

My journey in life is not yet complete, and I am experiencing profound joy in life and shifting to a new chapter in my personal life and professional life. The revelation that I was always worthy eluded me most of my life, and now I see that without going through this deep work each day, then all I could be would be adequate or average. I have a life that is full throttle and wide open. I look at each day with expectation and not dread. I don't ruminate about past failures, and it has enabled me to venture into starting my own business and be willing to adapt to changes that previously would have thrown me down the spiraling drain.

### Final Thoughts on Encouragement

I am grateful to you who have read through this work with me, as I have written my thoughts of encouragement for you. It is with profound gratitude that I share with you these final thoughts as you venture out to your day. You are enough! Often, I would hear and see this statement and think to myself, *What an absolute load of ...* Well, you get the picture. However, what I have come to learn is, this one statement fulfills the greatest spiritual gift that one can receive—peace. The peace that surpasses all understanding. The oneness that I feel with nature as I walk softly through the forest in late fall on a cool dew ladened trail. The scent, the sounds, and the interaction with the doe that allowed me near her with no fear. The gratitude that I felt for each of these moments.

The words have changed as well in my life from 'I have to' to 'I get to.' I am once again excited about learning through reading and listening to audiobooks, learning from others, reaching out, and writing. I find my greatest joy in writing as I do in this moment with you along with me. It is the realization that I am not alone; I have value, not because someone else values, but because I value who I am. You have a story, a journey, and a path that is in front of you to experience. It is not meant to be controlled; it is meant to be experienced. It is meant for you to sit and ask yourself "What is it that I need to learn from this experience?" and not ask "Why me?"

Let me provide one last illustration. In 2021, I had been thinking about establishing a life coaching and business transformation/improvement company. I was also evaluating whether or not I should move out of the country permanently. I met with my boss and shared with him my plans about establishing my company during my off hours as well as asking about moving. I shared my reasons for it and where I wanted to move to; his reaction was positive, and he asked that I explore it, and we would discuss it more. During this time, I began to pray about my decisions and the barriers that would prevent me from moving. Only two came to mind—money and a relationship. I was very specific about the type of partner I wanted in my life, and if that was not possible or manifested, I would happily leave the country and never come back.

I had actually met my girlfriend earlier in the year, but I did not feel I was in a place where my emotional and mental states were ready or prepared for any relationship. I took time off from dating altogether, and I also chose to live a life without alcohol. Well, the business startup costs were much more than I had anticipated, and the person that I wanted to share a life with that I had outlined in my prayers was and is now my girlfriend. I believe, had I not taken the steps I had to address the changes in my life and realize what could be, I would still be stuck in the same old, self-sabotaging victim mentality and quite possibly no longer living. Is change difficult? Yes, but what is even more difficult is waking up every day unchanged, with little, if any, hope and even less by doing nothing. Today, I choose to be happy, not because of my girlfriend but because I choose to be happy. It is not the uncontrollable laughter kind of happiness; it is the quiet confidence that I am happy because I am.

## About Brad Burchnell

Brad Burchnell is the founder and chief heartset officer/coach of From My Heart to Yours, LLC (www.fmhtyllc.com), located in Roseville, MI, where he provides his presence, compassion, empathy, intent, and integrity to assist his individual clients to realize a renewed heartset and mindset that leads them to a deep sense of peace and joy. His corporate client offerings include emotional intelligence training and business transformation for a healthier bottom line with improved employee engagement and participation. Brad has a diverse background of writing, collaborative efforts, and being featured in such works as:

1. *Journey Well; You are more than enough* by Mariah and Byron Edington

2. *Scars to Stars – Volume 2* by Deanna Mitchell

3. *Lightbulb Moments: Through the Eyes of Men – Terrifying, Traumatic, Triumphant - Stories of Hope.* A collection by Kerrie Atherton

4. *From My Heart To Yours – I am Not My Mistakes* by Brad Burchnell

5. Numerous podcasts and livestreaming events

He has served in leadership that includes serving in the US Navy as a chief petty officer in the field of meteorology and oceanography for 15 years, senior positions in manufacturing that included him serving as the onsite senior executive of a $4.5 million operation, and also serving as a leader and assistant leader of faith-based grief support for over seven years. He is a graduate of Fresno State University, where he received his bachelor's degree in industrial technology and manufacturing; he also did post-graduate work in the field of counseling from Trinity College of the Bible and Theological Seminary. He is blessed with a son-in-law married to his oldest surviving daughter and a grandson, and his youngest daughter is seeking a master's degree at Grand Rapids Theological Seminary.

CHAPTER 7

# Let Go and Let God

—

## Todd George Stone

I was born in Little Rock, Arkansas. My dad was a Southern Baptist preacher. My mother babysat in the home. I remember being a pretty happy child. When I was four, we moved to Lockesburg, Arkansas, because my dad was going to be pastoring a church in De Queen, Arkansas, just a few minutes away. The parsonage was a trailer on a bit of land. Everyone was coming by to meet the pastor and his wife and two small children. As a four-year-old, and my sister being just 13 months younger than me, we went to bed early. Sometimes, it was still daylight outside. People would come in and out, even while we slept, to take a peek at the pastor's children.

One evening, there were two men and a woman standing in my room. I thought I recognized the woman. I never met her, but I knew I was related to her. I will say that I always felt comforted by the people coming in. But when I turned to look again, they were gone. However, I still couldn't get the woman out of my mind. So, I ran down the hall to my mom. She asked if I needed a drink of water. I said, "No, where is the company?" She asked, "What company?" I replied, "The company that was just here. Who is that woman?" She again repeated, «There has been no one here … there has been no company." And I don't know how, at just four years of age, I knew, but I knew that I was seeing ghosts. After that, I started becoming fearful. I started to become a very nervous child, with migraine headaches, stomach problems, and nail-biting—which I still do today … still working on that.

By the time I started first grade, we moved back to Little Rock. It was then that I first heard derogatory slurs. I remember asking my mother one time when she was cooking dinner, although I don't remember which term I used, but it meant 'gay.' She explained to me what it meant, and I suddenly realized that's who I am, and it had a negative connotation to it. So, good Lord, at only six years old, I'm having to hide seeing spirits and being 'gay,' which had nothing to do with 'sex' at that time.

Throughout my school years, I had a lot of name-calling and bullying. At age 15, I realized these guys and girls were picking on me based on assumptions. So, I just came out. And that was hard in itself, but believe it or not, I had less trouble after I came out than before. I had taken their power away.

Ten years after graduation, with the invention of the internet, my class put together a type of chat room (before Facebook), and several of the bullies apologized to me. We do grow up a lot after high school.

During my 20s and 30s, my family started to come around, accepting me for who I am. There were still some hurdles to jump through, and I had several long-term relationships going into my 40s. And all this time, I keep repressing hearing from spirit. Hard to keep relationships going when they are not embraced by your family.

Then I fell in love with a narcissist. Also, he had unmedicated bipolar disorder. I never knew the clues to being in a narcissistic relationship, neither did I know what the word 'narcissist' meant. They put you on a pedestal, shower you with love, brag about you to other people, then suddenly pull it all away—all of it. They tell everyone it's all your fault, then they become the victim. Then it's make-up time! And the whole cycle starts again. And I don't know how, but I found myself absolutely still in love with him. I was deeply in love.

All appearances to the outside world were that everything was great, and we were meant to be together. On the inside, however, things would go from great to miserable if I just disagreed with him or if he just happened to have a bad day. He would get violent sometimes, and other times, he would just become silent and lock himself in the bedroom. I was constantly trying to smooth things out and calm the energy down. And when the final breakup between us happened, my spirit went completely dark. It was a total surprise. He suddenly just didn't want to be with me anymore. I was so depressed and actually became a loner for a while. I slept quite a bit, lived in my car off and on, and lost 25 pounds in less than a month. He even put an order of protection against me, making me look like I was a danger to him. He was a bit over 6ft. tall, and I'm 5'5. My doctor at the time said that I was having a 'nervous breakdown.' My ex took everything I owned, including clothes and even childhood trinkets. I got arrested once because he claimed I had violated the protection order. It was a lie, and my lawyer quickly bailed me out and had the charge dropped. He was determined to destroy me, but God had another plan.

The depression got deeper and darker, and this went on for months, and I was still completely in love with him, still thinking he would suddenly ask me back. And having my walls down, Spirit started coming through real strong. Oh Lord ... now I'm having to deal with this again! I kept hearing "Help others, and it will help you." My response was, "How am I supposed to help anyone else when I'm a horrible mess?" I had a friend that was delivering food and cigarettes, leaving them at my door because I wouldn't talk to anyone except through text. He suddenly had a trip planned to India. So, I had run out of everything and had to go to the store to re-stock. I forced myself to take a shower because I couldn't even stand the smell of myself. I still kept hearing "Help others, and it will help you." So, I went out to my car, and of course, it didn't start because I hadn't driven it in over a month. There was a neighbor that was outside; he asked if I needed a jump. After not seeing or talking to anyone in person for over a month, I had my first conversation. I said, "Yes, I guess I do, please.» He jumped my car, and I went to the closest store there was.

I walked into the store and got what I needed. I noticed the cashier had a beautiful ring on. I was so taken by this ring that I asked to get a good look at it. She obliged, and I told her, "That is the most beautiful setting I have ever seen. It must be an antique." She said, «Yes, it is. It was my grandmother's, and I just got it after she passed a few weeks ago. I have had it on ever since, and not one friend, family member, or coworker has noticed or said anything about it until you." Her eyes filled with tears, and the smile on her face was uplifting. As I walked out the door, God said, «See ... what did I tell you? If you help someone else, it will help you." I said, "God, really? Just a compliment?" And I heard a big 'YES' from God.

I slowly started to find a way to help uplift someone else sincerely every day. It was hard at first because I still wasn't in my 'right space' mentally, but I forced myself to find a way because, what did I have to lose? Nothing. I couldn't go any lower than I already was. It started to really feel good to make someone else happy again, and a lot of things started to change in my life.

It's about coming to the table with an 'attitude of gratitude'; about being grateful for what you do have; helping others, no matter where you are emotionally or physically, even with just a smile or kind words. I now know it's not just about me but about everyone else too. It's about collective consciousness. Together, we work to raise our own vibrations, and by doing this, we in turn raise the vibrations of the collective.

Now, Spirit has shown me how to use His voice to translate His messages through me to help others know they, too, are loved and supported. I had to 'let go and let God' to get to this place. And, of course, my religious family and friends didn't understand my spiritual journey. They are finally coming around again now because I have a half-sister that sees and hears Spirit like I do, and now, they have to pay attention.

'Let go and let God.' Even though that has become a phrase that has been used and abused, saying it and actually doing it has brought me to the best place I have ever been in my life. If you are having that tugging feeling in your heart gnawing away at you, well, just maybe you should listen to it because that is God leading you to a better place and time in your life too. With God at the helm, there is truly hope!

I decided to go with the flow of Spirit, although he moved me quickly to three different places that I swear I went kicking and screaming. I didn't want to go where I was being led but made a vow to myself that I would go wherever Spirit leads me, and I'm glad I did. I wouldn't be where I am now. I might not even still be here sharing this story of hope and faith in the yet-to-be-seen with you.

During this 'moving' time, God showed me more and more how to listen to Him to help others and show others the unconditional love of the universe. He moved me to a place with lots of love and light—more than I ever lost in any other relationship. A home that is paid for, with some land, and more material things than I can use. Seriously, we give things away all the time! A client/friend bought me a car and a phone. Friends have helped us tremendously. I did say 'we.' Yes, God brought me into a loving relationship that I also went kicking and screaming.

As Zechariah 4:10 in the Bible says, "Do not despise small beginnings." And never doubt where God is trying to lead you—from here to where you are truly meant to be.

### SEASONS OF HOPE

*Winter is not my favorite Season. Cold, dead, grey, and a lot of times just … dark.*

*I'm going through a winter in my soul. I've bundled up and layered up to the max to protect myself from all the dangerous, relentless elements …*

*But you have to be exposed enough to breathe and see, and those elements of a cruel season target where and when it can, trying to kill off anything exposed, as that is just the nature of the storm itself …*

*Doing its job in spite of any obstacles placed in its path.*

*But I remind myself of one thing; It's only ...*
    *a season.*

*Spring is on its way. New life and old life renewed. I remind myself that there is no hope without a loss, no profound joy without profound sadness, no faith without lingering doubt, and absolutely no resurrection without ...*
    *a death.*

*So, I let the season kill off what it needs and lay my hope and faith at my feet that no suffering will be in vain. And I wait ... till I see the first sign of green, the first bud, and then finally ... th*
    *a renewal.*

*And then the 'new season' reminds me that the sun the clouds have been hiding has been there all along ...*
    *a new season of hope.*

## About Todd George-Stone

I was born and raised in Little Rock, Arkansas. After graduation, I went to Cosmetology School and did hair for 35 years, even owning a salon for a while. During this time, I also raised exotic birds. From small finches and parakeets to even larger birds like parrots. I own an umbrella cockatoo that will be 18 years old in April 2023. If you didn't know, these big birds can live up to 80 or 100 years! She can be the life of any get-together, as cockatoos tend to demand attention and are the 'lap' birds of the parrot family.

I am also a singer, as a lot in my family are. My dad and half-sister play by ear; they can play almost any instrument and can write their own songs. I can sing, but I can't play anything but the radio. I found my first stage of course in church. My sister and I had a duo that was titled "Return to Grace." I have been privileged to meet some gospel legends, or I should say blessed to have met them.

I also was the general manager of a bar and grill that one of my sisters owned. A big career change, but it was one of my favorite jobs! The nights were late getting in, but the clientele made it worth it. It's actually where I met my best friend, and now we help each other through our spiritual journeys.

I am now a spiritual reader and life coach. I live out in the country in Lonoke, Arkansas, with my spouse Chris, two chihuahuas, a cockatoo, some outside cats, and some finches and fish. I guess I am starting a farm.

I anxiously await to see what God has in store for me next. Always remember that your story isn't finished yet. Have faith in the 'Yet to be seen,' and let go and let God!

# CHAPTER 8

# Change Doesn't Have an Expiration Date

———

Ipek Williamson

### I Love Fresh Lemons

When life brings us lemons, we make lemonade with them. But what if the lemons turned out to be spoiled, and their refreshing sourness became bitter? That might be the shortest and easiest way of describing what I experienced in the spring of my 48th year on this beautiful planet. And even though that experience hit me hard, I am acutely aware that it is nothing compared to much more dramatic and challenging situations millions of people are going through daily. But still, I want to share my story with you because I want to bring your attention to something that will encourage you if you think it is too late for you to make a significant change in your life or too hard to open a new chapter after being hit by a poisonous arrow.

### A Bit of Background

Before getting to the main story, I would like to tell you a little bit about myself. I have always been an overachiever, go-getter, multitasker, and perfectionist in all areas of my life. Many people described me countless times in my 20+ years of executive assistant career as an organized, proactive, responsible, trustworthy, curious, and creative person and employee. Being in charge, knowing what I am responsible for delivering, and having a clear direction always played a critical part in my success. Fairness, integrity, kindness, connection, and collaboration have always been my primary personal values. The environments where any of those is missing make me feel stressed and anxious.

Having shared this quick background about myself, let us scroll back to that hope-filled spring day.

## A Fresh Start

When you work for more than a few years anywhere, the job might become stagnant, repetitive, and boring sometimes. And at the organization I was working as the executive assistant to the president, I liked the people I worked with together. Though I was becoming more restless while my motivation and excitement were receding consistently.

One day, when I went to my personal email account to clean the spam messages crowding my inbox, I noticed a message that came through LinkedIn from an HR professional at a well-known local insurance company. She would like to connect with me. I went to LinkedIn and accepted her connection request. She sent me a message where she mentioned a senior executive assistant position in their organization that she was trying to fill and asked whether or not I would be interested in having a conversation about it. When I said "Okay," she set a time for the same afternoon, after work, to have a phone call with me.

The job was assisting the president of the company and managing three other executive assistants. The pay and benefits were better than I had at my then-current company; the office location was closer to home; the responsibilities were more elaborate; the position included managerial stature; and the number of people working for the company for 20+ years was quite impressive. They needed someone for that position, as the then-current senior executive assistant was about to retire.

I was excited about this opportunity falling into my lap. After three in-person interviews and saying goodbye to the manufacturing company I worked for previously, I took the job and started to work at this beautiful new office building. This position meant a new sector, a well-known company with a solid reputation, a female boss (a first for me), a managerial aspect added to my role, a new title, and better compensation. It all looked 'too good to be true.'

The start date of my new job was a beautiful sunny day in May. I was bringing with me 20+ years of experience, lots of self-confidence, and motivation.

**Or IS It?**

But things started to become weird fast. A week after I started working there, I discovered that the senior executive assistant who was supposed to retire was not going to do that until she turned 65, which would be four months later! That was very unusual.

Also, I could not get a minute of one-on-one time with my boss for a whole work week, even though she was in the office. Everything seemed to be so secretive. Gaining access to my boss's email account and monitoring her emails—one of the very basic tasks an assistant takes over rapidly—did not happen for several weeks. And receiving proper training from the senior executive assistant turned out to be wishful thinking. As someone who seeks clarity and direction, this was a very uncomfortable situation. My anxiety was literally over the roof. I ended up booking time on my boss's calendar to meet with her and review whatever little I was working on.

When I finally could speak with my boss, I voiced my concerns and asked for her help. I pleaded with her to include me in her closed-door meetings with her current assistant so that I could learn and understand her way of working. Although she seemed to agree with everything I said, she did not act upon any of the points I made. When that happened, the alarm bells in my mind were screaming loud and clear.

## What's Wrong?

There was something wrong. I could not get the information, insight, or knowledge to perform my job. There was no intention or action toward having me do what I was employed to do, but I was still hopeful that if I could be patient and wait for the current assistant to retire, everything would change, and I would be able to connect with my boss.

That treatment made me feel like a newbie, even though I had more than two decades of experience in my field. Because I was trying to do my job with only 10% of the information I needed, I made a few mistakes due to miscommunication, which created inappropriate and unfounded overreactions. I felt lost. I started to second-guess every work-related decision or action and worried about whether or not every little thing I did was good enough, correct, or acceptable.

I lost twelve pounds in two months. I was emotionally upset, anxious, and stressed daily from feeling invisible, left out, and not accepted by the team. Looking back at the course of events while wearing my coaching hat, I can see clearly. When you join any team, group, or collective, you look at establishing a state of belonging. You feel connected and happily contribute toward the greater good when you truly belong. The sense of belonging in that environment did not represent itself to me. And that was leading me at light speed toward a full-blown depression.

I started this job thinking I brought a new and improved set of eyes, with a more analytical and better technological skill set that was acutely missing in the office. So, I was excited about the contributions I planned to make in bettering the top-level administrative processes. But what I faced, instead, was to sit at my desk and play the junior assistant to the senior executive assistant for four months.

## Keeping A Secret- Hoping It Will Get Better

I was not sharing any of this with my husband, Craig. He was also laid off from work at the time and was working on finding a job for himself.

I did not want to add more stress to his plate by telling him everything I was going through at work. I wanted to spare him my sadness, disappointment, and anger. My rationale for doing this was assuming it was just a matter of time. Maybe I would have to wait four months to get where I would be by myself and create my autonomy, but it was still okay. I was going to be patient. It was not a big deal not being trained or guided. After all, I was not learning to swim after jumping into dark waters without a lifeline for the first time. I never got anyone showing me the ropes for more than a few days at any of my previous workplaces. So, I was going to be okay as soon as I took over the reins. And later on, when I told him everything about this, we would laugh about it.

Exactly two months after my employment started at the company, I left to go to Turkey for two weeks. That was a condition I negotiated before taking the job and accepted by my boss—as I had booked my flights many months before this job change. Generally, this should have been a happy event for me! However, during this visit with my family and friends that I was looking so forward to, I felt anxious and worried about my new job the whole time. And the trip turned out to be torture for me. I could not sleep, eat, or enjoy any part of it. And for the first time in my life, I did not want to return to Canada.

I went to the airport to take my return flight, which ended up being delayed four hours. While waiting to board my plane, I started to cry. I knew what was waiting for me was not anything pleasant.

## The Shock!

The first day going back to the office was really hard. Still, I could manage to get through it. But the next day, exactly two weeks before the end of my probation period, when I went to the office, I saw my boss and the VP of HR in her office. No one else was in yet, as it was still quite early.

My boss called me into her office and said that I was not the right fit for the position and that they would have to let me go. Then she left the office, and the building, leaving me in her office with the VP of HR, who resumed explaining to me what was next. She was talking to me, but I could not hear her. All the feelings of shame, anger, disappointment, confusion, despair, and fear were hitting me at once. I felt crushed into pieces. In all the years as an executive assistant, I have never had such an experience.

Now, looking back, I see myself immediately taking the victim role. I remember the questions that were rushing to my mind. Why was that happening to me? What did I do wrong? Why would they pull me out of my previous job and hire me, only to fire me right before the end of the probation period? Did the retiring assistant change her mind and decide to stay, and now I was redundant? Or was I a real loser? But I had an exemplary track record with all my previous employers. How could I have changed this drastically within a few months? I couldn't stop my mind from constantly thinking about this. The room was spinning around me. The VP of HR told me to gather my things, and even before other people started to come to the office, I left for good.

## Learning What an Ego Death Is

After this unprecedented event, I was in shock for quite a long time. I was worried that it would affect my employability. What would the representatives of the companies I applied to think when they noticed my work with my last employer was less than three months? How would I be able to explain that? I had so many concerns and fear about the future of my career, but I didn't have time to mourn. I needed the income. So, I immediately started to look for temporary jobs, and I ended up working at two extraordinary workplaces back-to-back. As if the universe was trying to make up for my unfortunate experience, people were kind and friendly to me, and the work was interesting at both workplaces.

Despite the warmer welcomes and better work environments, I still felt low, depressed, unworthy, not enough, and not deserving. In the meantime, my husband and I decided to sell our house in Kitchener, Ontario, and move to Sarnia, Ontario, where my husband's two siblings and memories from his childhood lived.

Sarnia is a small but mighty city sharing a border with Michigan, US. It has a beautiful beach by Lake Huron, parks, and streets filled with old and magnificent trees. We found our happy home in this cute little city. Our lovely and cozy house is also small but mighty, while our happiness is big and bubbly.

The move to Sarnia came like a lifesaver to me. As I knew we were going to move, I did not look for a permanent job, instead preferred temporary jobs. But now that the move was complete, it was time for me to search for a permanent executive assistant position. I applied to a few and even had a few interviews, but before every interview, I felt the same anxiety, nausea, and panic. After refusing a couple of job offers with unfounded excuses, I knew it was time to be honest with myself and admit that my career as an executive assistant was over. It was time for me to accept that the negative experience I went through ended my career as an executive assistant. It hurt my self-confidence and self-worth so massively that I could never recover from it.

## Now What?

When I realized and accepted that fact, I started thinking about what to do. I was not going back to a full-time job in a corporate setting. That part was obvious to me. I started looking for less stressful, part-time jobs, which I soon enough found. Four days a week reception job at a dental office located three minutes from my home. That job gave me the belonging feeling that I needed badly. It was a lovely, family-like atmosphere, a position with fewer responsibilities and a clearer mind with open space to create new ideas. In the meantime, I was meditating, journaling, blogging, reading, exploring, learning, and growing. I was trying to find my 'why, how, and when.'

On October 28, 2019, my 50th birthday, me, my husband Craig, my son Ali, and my father Ümit went to have dinner and celebrate this important milestone. My father was visiting us from Turkey at the time. That night, after a delicious dinner, the waiter brought a birthday cake with five candles on it. And before blowing the candles, I made a promise instead of a wish. I said, "From this moment on, I will only do the things that give me joy."

After that day and in due time, all the answers started to show up on my path. I knew that I had a strong desire to help others. I have always been a compassionate, resourceful, practical person focused on being proactive rather than reactive. I was also discovering the immense positive effects of meditation through practicing it religiously and learning more and more about it. So, I realized through careful soul-searching and literal, real-life research that coaching and teaching meditation were my sources of joy.

While working part-time, I also began receiving training in coaching and meditation. During the training periods and after my graduation, I relentlessly practiced. Then, slowly but surely, clients started to come my way. Opportunities, collaborations, and projects began to materialize. It took me three full years to get to the level where I became confident and resourceful within my practices as an insight coach and meditation teacher. And despite many ups and downs and a pandemic that shook the world to its magma, I got there. With my amazing husband's support and encouragement, I bit the bullet. I decided to quit my day job and devote all my time and energy to my new and blooming practice. It was time to devote my undivided focus to coaching and meditation practices where I would make a difference for many. I left my desk to my lovely predecessor and came home.

### It's A New Dawn; It's A New Day; It's A New Life for Me—And I'm Feeling Good!

I spruced up my home office. I turned the room into a cozy and comfortable place to have coaching sessions, online workshops, meditations, and calls with my colleagues and friends.

I am in my office for several hours every day, but because everything I do gives me joy, excitement, and happiness, I don't see it as work. I see it as transformation, growth, evolution, expansion, joy-creation, and fulfillment not only for me but also for everyone who shows up in my day, in my office, in person or online. And I love every minute of it. My office is my sanctuary. Some days I light candles or incense, and on other days I use my essential oil diffuser while working or practicing my daily meditations. I get to be me in 'my office.' Also, I spend lots and lots of quality time with my amazing husband and all my other loved ones. Enjoying life, enjoying myself and my relationships while doing good in the world to the best of my ability.

I get to look at my north star, which is joy, every day and ask myself if anything coming my way as a coach, meditation teacher, speaker, or author will potentially bring that into my life. If my intuition says yes—and believe me, I learned to listen to my gut the hard way—I say yes.

I realized that making lemonade with those lemons was not an option if I wanted to be mentally and physically healthy in the future. So, I took those bitter and spoiled lemons and threw them into the trash can.

**What's In It for You?**

Dear reader, I shared my story here to remind you that your life is the sum of your choices. Make sure you don't lean toward making choices where you see the least resistance, but rather, make your choices considering the joy and happiness they will bring you and everyone around you.

I can say with certainty and from experience that when you do anything with passion, determination, love, and intention of serving, helping, and creating, you cannot fail in the long run, even if you try to. I am the proof of it. This book you are reading right now is proof of it.

You have what it takes within you to recreate, rebuild, and renovate your life every day. By waking up, you get the chance to create yourself and everyone else around you every day. It is like winning the lottery every day. You have a blank canvas that you can fill with as many colors as you like. Choosing darker colors or cheerful, joyful, lively ones is up to you. Life is beautiful, and it is trying to show its beauty to you daily through the beauty of nature, friendships, and little pleasures. Do not consume them as you do with social media. Savor them. If at 50 I could start a new life, a new and successful career, you certainly can do the same and even more.

Believe in yourself, find your passion, and make your life yours. If you are still okay with making lemonades, then be happy with that choice, but make sure it is your choice.

**Discussion Questions:**

1. What is the most significant change that you have experienced in your life?

2. Was the change decision yours, or was it initiated by others?

3. How did that change affect your life?

4. On a scale of one (least) and seven (most), how happy are you at work? If your score is closer to 'least' on the scale, what can you do to improve it?

5. On a scale of one (least) and seven (most), how happy are you in your personal life? If your score is closer to 'least' on the scale, what can you do to improve it?

6. In a perfect world, what would your work and personal life look like?

7. What small change could you make today in your life that would raise your levels of energy, happiness, and joy?

## About Ipek Williamson

Ipek Williamson is the founder and CEO of Ipek Williamson Coaching. She is a change master, listener, certified insight coach, speaker, author, Ikigai and Ho'oponopono practitioner, and meditation advocate & teacher.

She perfectly blends her 20+ years of corporate experience with diversified areas of expertise as a coach, mentor, and teacher.

Ipek intends to help anyone and any relationship that needs healing and improvement, especially relationship with oneself.

In addition to her multiple highly acclaimed meditations that she showcases through the Insight Timer app, Ipek leads live meditation sessions through that same application. She also offers group coaching, workshops, courses, and training to teams and corporations.

CHAPTER 9

# Breaking Free - Out of Darkness

———

## Karen Ortega

Years ago, as a child, I experienced sibling abuse and was molested by several cousins. I was born a sensitive, tender-hearted child, and these experiences devalued my sense of self, and consequently, I struggled with this for years.

We lived on a big, beautiful farm in Missouri, where, as a child, I found peace and solace. It was wide open; I felt free and explored every bit of this magical place. I connected very deeply with the farm, and animals were an added benefit. Sneaking past a herd of cows with a bull hanging out was daring but fun ... Somehow, we had these really tall hogs that my sister and I were terrified of. My dad would later say they were some type of hybrid ... I remember my sister throwing out the leftover dinner and dropping the bowl into the slurry of grunting hogs. She immediately ran, screaming into the house, and my ass, as big sister, had to climb the gate and grab the bowl once these pigs meandered off, or risk getting in trouble. I was brave and scurried over the gate, grabbed the bowl, and pretty much dived back over the gate to safety in two seconds flat; those neanderthal pigs heard me and were rushing back, thinking I had more goodies ... Tall pigs running and grunting toward you. Pretty scary!

I did plenty of brave things in those days. Looking back now, I was much braver than I gave myself credit for. It takes bravery to jump out of a barn loft 10 ft down. It takes bravery to explore the dark recesses of that big old barn or run through a field toward a row of large round hay bales, unsure what type of farm animal was in that pasture. But we were safe high up on those bales; it felt like a mountaintop. Life was daring and fun outside, and all of my spare time was spent there.

During the time of sibling abuse, I felt alone and unprotected, not brave at all, as both of my parents worked, and sibling abuse rarely happens in the presence of adults. I made myself scarce when *he* was around. I hid and tried to make myself unseen and unheard in an attempt to avoid his piercing hate-filled words and sudden bursts of anger for no reason to slam me against the wall. It was a hatred that, as a child, I never understood. I remember my very first traumatic experience with my brother at the age of around four. My mom had set up a kiddie pool for my brother, and while we splashed, I remember my brother suddenly reaching over, grabbing my neck, and trying to hold my head under the water. I had to fight to get him to let go. It terrified me. It was my first moment to experience a real fear of death. I ran, screaming in terror, to our mom, who had been in the house. I remember her coming, running toward me, but the memory fades after that ...

My parents would have big family gatherings on the farm with hayrides and barn tunnels made with hay bales that the older cousins would make. We had barbecues and an amazing family atmosphere, except for the cousins, who were much older and molested several of us by coaxing us at five to sit in their lap to read a book and then touch us where they shouldn't.

I remember feeling confused and not liking it at all. And also, being a very young child not knowing what to do, it happened several times at different gatherings, ending in one cousin calling me upstairs and asking me to pull down my pants to show him my *parts*. And he'd show me, except he already pulled down his pants and was standing in front of me naked, proudly showing me his penis. Thankfully, I had the sense to run away and down the stairs.

I was embarrassed and confused and never told my parents. It was a secret that I only told one cousin who happened to be the other molester. I remember him smiling as he coaxed it out of me. I wondered why he was smiling while I clung to and fidgeted with a bush as I told him the best way a five-year-old could—that his brother pulled out his 'peepee' and showed it to me. I remember being afraid as I talked and the reason I was hiding behind the bush.

Maybe I had PTSD at an early age. I was a nervous child who hated loud noises and would run to another room or outside, even when the vacuum cleaner came on. It was probably made worse by my mom sucking up a marble or two; my dad would say she'd go through vacuums twice a year. Noises and sudden, unexpected moments jolt me with anxiety and pierce me to this day.

I remember only a few times my brother getting caught being abusive to my sister and me, and the punishment by our dad was swift, but it did not lessen the abuse. He would just become more careful.

My eighth-grade dance came, and my mom told my brother to take me. He was angry and didn't want to, but she made him. He was 16, and I was 14. The amount of verbal abuse and hate that spewed forth on that car ride was felt in such a way that I felt pieces of me literally slipping away. He raged in a seething, hostile way about how much he hated me. I was the ugliest, most vile thing to him in that moment, and he refused to drop me off in front of the dance hall because he would say he wouldn't be caught dead with me. He dropped me off a block away and instructed me to meet him in a far-away parking lot after the dance—all because he refused to pull up and be seen with me. But after the dance, I pretended to not see his flashing lights, and he was forced to come and get me, which infuriated him. I endured a barrage of hate and more silence as I looked out the window, trying to tune him out. I did not tell my parents. I suppose I knew what the consequences would be the next time we were alone. Maybe I thought they wouldn't believe me.

I watched my brother thrash my sister around in the swimming pool on a few occasions, and the violence that was veiled in play scared the hell out of me. I remember him standing on her back underwater, not letting her up. A neighbor who was present screamed at him to let her up, saying he was going to drown her.

I was aware of the exact time he would be coming home, and as soon as I saw his car coming down the road, I would promptly exit the pool and go inside to the 'relative safety' of the house. Time seemed irrelevant, but I was highly mindful and on alert constantly. I think this is what probably led to PTSD.

I lived in that sense of fear all those years. My first marriage at the age of 15 was also abusive. I ran from one abuser to another unknowingly, and it was a long way back to myself over the years. It was easy for someone to say they loved me, and I would happily go on, thinking it would be better. The grass was greener, or so I thought, but I learned real quick that it wasn't, and more of the same ensued. Men tell me they love me, but then they don't … not really. I guess that this is the lead-up to learning finally to love myself.

I did not at all have a sense of self-worth or what 'real love' felt like. Our parents had a love-hate relationship, so that is what seemed 'normal' to me. I knew what emotional as well as physical abuse was from an early age because it was what my childhood was entwined with.

It wasn't always bad. Our brother played tricks and jokes on us that were funny, but the times when the abuse happened overshadowed the good times because I felt that abuse to my core, and it stayed with me deep inside for years. There is a deep sadness that comes with psychological, emotional, or mental abuse. Yet, until you recognize what it is, you will continue to stay in it and end up going to the lowest and darkest places.

For years, in my marriages, I had no idea what 'narcissistic abuse' even was. I had no idea that what I was experiencing was, in fact, psychological abuse. There is a devaluing stage in relationships, and then the loving stage; both are cycles in an endless loop. To someone who has no hope, it's a relentless cruel game to no end. The hurts that come set you back again and again. Then the love that is shown gives you 'false hope' but only lasts a short while. It's never on a continuum, just a roller coaster that you feel you can't get off because you still don't understand the underlying message that this isn't 'real love.'

My quiet, extraordinarily shy self left at some point. I think this was a good thing. It was replaced with anger and rage. Then, in the rage, I started to find myself as I dealt with the anger I was now feeling after figuring out what I had allowed to happen to me. In the deeper recesses of myself, I found the strength to pull myself back. I called all of those shattered pieces back. It was through Tarot, books like *Unshakeable Power* by Char Murphy, friends, family, YouTube, and through my own inner knowing that was guiding me.

I started to listen, even if I was told I was wrong or just trying to fit into a narrative. It was a multitude of things, but when I started listening and noticing the repetitive messages, things started to change, and this time, I was determined to finally stand up for myself and what I knew to be true. I trusted myself more and more, and my world started to change almost magically and immediately after that.

It took yet another person with strong narcissistic traits again to show me the lesson because my stubbornness to learn is massive. I learned a lot from this one. I struggled so much with this one. I struggled to be with him; I struggled to trust him; I struggled to detach; I struggled to undo from him. I saw his good; I saw his bad; I saw his gentleness sometimes. I saw how much he cared by helping me, but I also experienced the gaslighting, lies, deflecting, withholding … and the dance in and out of the flame. I stood by and watched him choose his passive-aggressive and demanding family members over and over again. I felt abandoned and betrayed, but something else in me was growing. It was deeply wounding for me to feel rejected, but at the same time, I stood my ground, knowing I had the right to, and this was healing for me.

This was also the start of me realizing something was really off. I knew that he wasn't listening; I wasn't feeling heard or seen; my feelings were being ignored and passed over for the greater good of the 'group' and those who wanted control. I couldn't understand; this felt so backward to me. Where is freedom? Why do we have to conform? However, I stayed because I wanted to fix it and him because I loved who I thought he could be, but something was missing, and I sure didn't feel like his queen.

I also had to deal with my own rage and reactive abuse. Several things brought me out of the dark. Educating myself about my own trauma of childhood abuse, marital abuse, and what PTSD feels like; it was a relief to understand I wasn't 'crazy.' I needed balance and someone who understood and could hold a space for me to grieve all the dark places I lived in for so long so I could let it all go. And that was ultimately just me because there was no one else standing beside me who could do that for me; it was just me. Even though my family backed me 100%,

I had to do all the heavy work, and part of that was grieving this man I wanted so much to be authentic and real, but he couldn't. His own trauma and denial of that kept him at arm's length. I dove in and out of forgiveness. I begged and pleaded for changes or apologies, anything, but they did not come. I would stare at the photo of his adorable two-year-old self and plead for him to come to me in a better way. I asked for mercy for us both; I prayed for help, guidance, and healing for both of us. Finally, I asked that we both be shown what was best for each of us, and the answer was always the same: "Let him go."

There was a deep healing happening, but it was also devastating. It was like my inner child was throwing a fit at the changes that were on the horizon. It was bittersweet; it was heartbreaking, but it was also the only way for me to heal and be truly happy. What I also knew and struggled with was knowing I deserved to be held within a family that respected and loved me authentically and unconditionally, and it wasn't them. I knew I would forever be the 'black sheep.' I knew that even with the circumstances and gift of reflection, he would be made to choose either them or me, and family is everything to him. Even if it is not always respectful, I knew in my heart he would choose that.

---

I chose to leave behind all of the toxic energy. It was heartbreaking to not be allowed to be fully embraced by others but also necessary for me to choose a higher level of calling and maybe someday 'my person.' It took 10 years for me to find my self-worth, and on a spiritual level, I knew that that's what he and his family were somehow teaching me.

I have been walking through forgiving myself for any harm I caused through my own triggers. I profusely apologized to him for the rage and my loss of control. I don't think a cross and holy water are needed anymore. I learned to surrender and let go of wanting things to be different. They couldn't be because I wouldn't have learned the lessons in forgiving myself and the reflection of my childhood I so desperately needed to let go of if it wasn't this way.

All the abuse may have shaped me, but it does not define me. I will always have a tender heart and a love for people who are hurt too. I know how much 'hurt people' can hurt others. I wish I had a magic wand to help everyone, but everyone has their own travels and unraveling to do for their own healing, and it's not for me to fix anymore. People can only fix themselves; I learned the hard way.

I am sure my angels who watch over me tediously and wide-eyed are breathing a sigh of relief and hallelujah-ing all over the place! It was a hard lesson—not having a loving, protective brother. There was a sense of loss, betrayal, and depression in that. I was always feeling like I carried a shield, and my first experience with the male ego formed how I would learn and even expect to be treated.

Now that we are older, I understand through a medium that my brother's anger was set in place by something that happened as I was presented to him and took the slot of the 'second child.' As we aged, a warmness grew between us that I felt; it hasn't so far been a close bond, but I have forgiven him, and I have been walking through the fire of releasing what-ifs and wishing it were different. From that perspective, it couldn't have been any different, or I wouldn't be writing this right now.

Our dad died a few years ago, and with all of us together, I felt my brother's love for once in my whole life. I felt his gratitude and love while I was there, helping our dad pass. It was a deep emotional wound that released and helped free me from the darkness. My brother was and is a great uncle to my sister and my kids.

Gone are the bad memories, and now I choose to remember the good ones. Sleigh riding down a hill in front of our farmhouse as siblings, plowing headfirst into the deep snowbanks. My brother on Halloween night waving a sheet outside my bedroom window as my best friend and I sat engrossed and in fear as we watched a scary movie. There were good times, and I will keep remembering them.

For all those years, I had no idea what a 'narcissistic abuse cycle' was or that I was embedded in one. I was so used to abuse from an early age that it was impossible for me to know it wasn't healthy to cry and rage over neglectful, avoidant, and dismissive people. I didn't understand that not feeling heard or seen was part and parcel of neglect and abuse, even in adult relationships. It is called 'bread crumbing' for a reason: barely giving anything but just enough to keep you hanging on and staying in the cycle.

I finally understood over the last year that no amount of crying or primal screams would change anything. No apologies were coming. I remember him saying that I wanted a bleeding-heart apology from his mother. "No," I said, "just hoped for a heartfelt apology for the cruel words said." She had always told me that she loved me, so the pain of silence and no remorse was deeply felt. There was that maddening silence, and there was also a fierce protectiveness in him that I never saw or felt. No apology ever came, and there was that stark utter silence. It was also that lesson again of self-worth and self-love. Is this good for me? Is this best for me? There was a lesson in standing up for myself and loving and respecting who I am, my beliefs, and my values. I stayed standing, as hurtful as it was. It felt so abnormal and far removed from the way I was raised, and as much as I wanted it to all fit nicely and fit in, I just didn't fit that mold. It felt to me like a sticky web, and I felt like I was the square peg trying to fit into a round hole.

I was silenced for 10 years. I wasn't allowed to speak up. I wasn't allowed to set boundaries or challenge anyone who infringed on my freedom. In fact, in one instance, I was accused, by the matriarch, of having a fling with his brother in the middle of a family dinner. The silence was deafening; not a word was uttered from either son, and dinner went on as if nothing was ever said. I even went on and continued to love this lady, not knowing the deeper issue at hand. I sat wide-eyed at that table in disbelief at all of them; I wanted to scream at her for such a manipulating comment, but I didn't. I pretended it didn't hurt. What I didn't realize is that I was enabling them to manipulate me. I was enabling them to treat me this way. I was, over time, conditioned to silence just as these boys were.

I was not going to be silenced, though. I took the long way around back to myself and faced them head-on. When I chose to stand my ground, it was the beginning of the end. I started to wake up more and more. I started coming back to myself. It was then that the lesson was integrated. I began to see myself differently. It still broke my heart to not feel safe and protected. I just wanted to feel emotionally safe. I wanted the same fierce protection but for integrity, not enabling. My heart needed to feel safe and held. I wasn't getting that, and I never would in this relationship. People can only do what they are capable of doing, given their own circumstances.

My capacity to still see through the eyes of love is my 'superpower,' and no one can ever take that from me. I think my incredible love for animals has kept me open to being a loving person all these years. And to be honest, I still struggle with trying to stabilize myself during trying times. Sometimes I think people are lying or hiding something from me when they are not. My ability to trust others has been shaken to my core, and I hope that will change with the right circumstances someday.

My next chapter has started. In my little, low-income apartment, I write this to say that I have become what I never thought I could or would be—strong enough to be standing here now, loving my freedom, learning to love myself and all the darkness, continuing to release day by day everything I have carried for so long. I have carried the world on my shoulders long enough. I now know I deserve big love; I deserve truth, honesty, transparency, and authenticity. I deserve the best. I have drawn closer to myself, and in doing that, I began to trust myself in all that I do. I feel more at peace now, and that is worth everything. There may always be a little fear, but it moves me forward, and that's just what I have to do for myself—inch past it and grow!

Always have the courage to 'see' what you don't want to. Trust and believe in yourself. Everything inside you will guide you. Listen to that inner voice. Watch for signs; don't give up. You may want to, but don't. Trust the universe. You are definitely loved and worthy of love!

"Healing takes courage, and we all have courage, even if we have to dig a little to find it."

—*Tori Amos*

## About Karen Ortega

Karen Ortega is a Missouri native who lived much of her life on a farm with her parents and two siblings north of St. Louis. It was a magical time for her, and the memories are rich and full of color. The farm she grew up on would always hold special memories—farm animals, family gatherings, hayrides, scary pigs, her beloved pets playing in the barn, and exploring from morning to night.

Karen's love for animals and nature is probably one of her greatest joys. Children also have always been a big part of her life, and she enjoyed the time she had raising her own children as well as several grandchildren that are under her wing now.

As Karen reached a point in her life where her two granddaughters were reaching adulthood status, she was on the cusp of knowing a freedom she hasn't known before. Raising kids is all she has ever known, and it's now her time to go to the next level and be solidly herself.

Although her educational level is minimal, no education could ever compare to the knowledge Karen has gathered along the way. She believes her time is now, and she hopes those who read what she has to say would gain the wisdom and courage to be who they are and be successful at simply that; anything that follows is for the greater good of everyone. Her prayer is for her readers to be blessed with the willingness to be their authentic selves in everything they do.

Karen dedicates this chapter to her son Dylan Ortega, who was with her and supported her the whole way, and to her granddaughter Destiny whose story is mentioned here too. She is grateful for the bond they shared even in the teenage ups and downs, which will never be broken. She is grateful to her family and friends and all the experiences that shaped her into her almost polished self today.

# CHAPTER 10

# Born Into Chaos

—

### Destiny Bogan

My name is Destiny, but people call me 'Dezz.' I was born into chaos. From the time I came out into the world, family battles have been all around me. My parents basically kidnapped me from each other, each doing what they thought was best for me. Then my sister came into the world a year later. I am 17 years old, two months shy of 18. If I had told myself 11 years ago that I would be here, 'she' would be confused and shocked. I never thought that I would get myself out of the situation I was put in at such a young age. I never truly met the world at six years old. Yet, I saw such an ugly part of it. But as I grew older, I knew … that doesn't define me.

I have an off-and-on relationship with my parents. Now they have their lives together and a more established way of living, and so do I. Living 12 hours away from them kind of made it harder to form a proper relationship, but I sometimes think of it as the best for me.

In the end, my mom won against my dad, but she wasn't really the true winner. Living with my mom overall was okay, but she was in a tight spot herself. She didn't have the means or spirit to take care of a kid at 23. I was mostly caring for my sister. My little clumsy hands doing the best I could to make my three-year-old sister a peanut butter sandwich or some cereal, accidentally pouring the milk all over the floor. My older cousin around the same age as my mom would come in and see us, as my mom was not paying attention—she was rather doing some frisky things with a guy. She would take us to McDonald's immediately. Just a little while later, mom met a guy who was really sweet at first, but something clicked a few months later. After moving in, he began to get more and more aggressive until, eventually, it was aimed at me and my sister. Like a lion killing a child that isn't his, he was beating us to a pulp for anything and everything. I remember a lot of key memories from that time, but the main thing I always thought was: that was my life—I had no other choice. And he would beat me for the rest of my life.

My family outside of us knew something 'awful' was going on, as they described it. When we were near the guy while we were at my family's house, we seemed genuinely terrified of him. Two years later, my brother was born. At that point, things were going south, as he was beating me to black and blue colors, and then … I woke up to someone touching me at night in places they don't belong. Having the human instinct at six years old to grab a knife and direct it toward his skin, I still never thought anything was wrong; it just felt unsafe and bad. Sneaking out at night to grab food cause I was so hungry; being in a sketchy neighborhood on top of it all. And no matter what, for saying my ABCs wrong, for saying the word horsey or calling him daddy, etc., I deserved a brutal beating. Even saying I had a boyfriend in kindergarten got me a hard slap across the face.

Eventually, CPS came for the hundredth time, and my mom told them everything. The cops told me that they had him just sitting on his hands; now I know he was sitting in handcuffs. I asked my great-grandpa when I was nine if he went to prison, because I heard them talking about it, and he just said, "Yeah, I think so." I still don't know for sure, and I don't want to ask.

This guy had a little brother who was around 15 when I was young. He had 'eyes for me.' He would ask me if he could practice kissing me for his girlfriend and if I wanted to have an idea of what a tongue felt like. I blocked that memory out for a long time, though, when I thought of the guy's older brother, who was very sweet and loving toward me and my sister. I realize it was the one light in the dark I had at that time.

After 12 years of therapy and several prescribed medications I was forced to take from six to 12 years old, I would ask the same questions to the universe, "Why me? Why did you have to take my childhood? Why do I have to be the kid who is 'mature' for her age?" When I turned 15, the universe answered, "Because this is you; this is what makes or breaks you. Learn, grow, and prosper."

The years of therapy and medication didn't fix the trauma I endured. It felt like nobody had gone through what I had—the built-up confusion and anger. And the medication never stopped the questions. At 12, I moved from my great-grandma's care to my maternal grandma's. She saw how the medication made me slow and tired and eventually stopped giving it to me but continued with therapy. She knew I was strong and could do it on my own with watchful, caring eyes and a heart to help me. She knew what I would become; she had faith in me. She called it her intuition, her 'gut feeling.' I felt the best I ever could, more energized and happier, but then, I crashed again. For me, it was like a rollercoaster. I was happy one moment, and then, the next, I felt like the world was trying to swallow me whole.

Back when I lived in my home state, I found out my great-grandpa had lung cancer. I was young and did not understand the circumstances, how it was terminal cancer, or what that really meant. My grandpa was my best friend, and I didn't understand the concept of death yet. He told me he hoped he could see me at my wedding and live to see my kids. My young mind turned his hope into a promise. A year after, I moved again, 12 hours away; we had received the worst call. We needed to drive there to see him one last time. I didn't understand the dire situation. I spent those nights sleeping with my great grandma so she wouldn't feel alone while he was in his hospice bed. The second night, he passed away in the same room as me an hour after I fell asleep. My world shattered again. It took me a moment, and then I realized I would never see his face again for the rest of my life. My hero, the man who took me out of my abusive household, was now with the universe.

I learned independence after that and controlled my anger and emotions, but the adult who caused my life to be so shambled from the start shook it again by starting a whole other new life with my main abuser, randomly shocking us all with the news of the family they had started without me. Not helping or caring, just a simple "I'm sorry for what I did to you" was all I got. I was always put to the side by that adult, always house-jumping. I still have fond memories of my earlier years when I was with my maternal grandma, especially when she put her foot down and said, "Give her to me for now." I was only four years old.

I knew that I could, in fact, do things on my own and that just because they are an 'adult' does not mean that they will keep you fully out of harm's way. I grew up in the harshest part of the world without a father and partially without a mother. My father then later tried to show up in my life at 10 years old through visitation, which did not end well. At 15, I made a decision that made my grandma upset and worried—I contacted my father through social media on the condition that if he left again, then I won't be coming back to him. He then made an effort, which slightly relieved me, her, and the rest of my family.

I learned forgiveness, allowing myself to make more room in my heart for growth. I moved forward, got a scholarship, set my final path, and declared to myself that I—yes, I—will be the most successful person in my family. I turned my torment into pride and gold. Every obstacle overturned. I am most grateful to my grandma for being there for me every step of the way. I knew that I was the only thing stopping me, and there is still stuff I try to get past every now and then. Some say that those so young haven't made many major achievements, but I have. I have seen the worst in my life, yet here I am. I would say that is a pretty big achievement in my book. I was asked at a young age, "Will you be a victim or a survivor? Will you resent all your life and be in misery? Or will you choose to be something better?" Well, I can definitely be something better, if not greater.

I sucked my fingers—from when I was a toddler to when I was 11 years old—for comfort from my trauma. I was most definitely bullied for it, and it definitely did not help that I refused to take a shower because I felt disgusted with my own body. Adding gas to a fire, I was fairly depressed and traumatized but vented that with anger at the time. I was just as confused as everyone else about why it was happening. I couldn't control what I was feeling or see that what I was doing was wrong.

Here enters a new family member that contributed to a bit of my trauma. But to this day, I don't speak to them, and I have mixed feelings toward them. They handled my emotional state wrong and messed with my mind quite a bit. They admitted that I was a traumatized kid, but when I would throw a fit at nine years old, it turned into boot camp. Not even forgetting when they would threaten me with a foster home whilst showing me videos on how bad foster homes can be and proceeding to make me pack my stuff myself and wait at the door (about a million times). But, at the same time, I can never fully blame them. Who knows how to take care of an emotionally scared kid properly? Not many. They tried multiple ways to get me to stop sucking my fingers; cayenne pepper was one of many. It never worked. Only I could stop myself, and as I aged, I slowly let go of what was behind me.

I was severely sheltered and protected for many obvious reasons. Sometimes I am thankful because I got to play outside instead of on my phone 24/7 like most of the kids my age, but I wore childlike clothes until I was 15 because I couldn't find myself. I was not allowed to go out with friends until 13, and I could only use natural eyeshadow at 12. No heels, not even an inch. I didn't know things like other kids did. At 12 years old, I didn't even know what the word 'president' meant. Again, some things were for the greater good, but my friends would treat me like an 'alien' because all I knew was 'play outside and school.'

Moving to my maternal grandmother's, like I will always say, was the best thing that could ever happen to me. She introduced me to spiritualism, something my family never told me about, as they were skeptics. She made me read those boring books on how to heal your soul. She bought me actual teenage clothes and let me use her makeup and her heels. I wore a jacket almost all my childhood, and my aunt and great-grandmother used to tell me to take it off, as it 'looked bad' on the clothes. But my grandmother, instead of making me feel vulnerable, gave me my confidence back by allowing me to know and feel like myself. She let me hang out with my friends every weekend and gave me the boost I needed. Now, I was rocketing to the moon. She said, "Hey, I think a nose piercing would look great on you," and on my next birthday, I got my nose pierced and loved it.

With every rise came a fall. My grandma and I got into arguments a lot. I was starting to act like my parents when they were rebellious. I got my long-term boyfriend at 15; we're currently still together—almost three years. He was 16. I would have shaken at the thought of sneaking out before, but being with him gave me a little more confidence. I usually snuck him in almost every night because I was scared to leave my home. I once tried to take my life when I got into a depressed episode. I was 'baker-acted.' The entire time, my grandma and I were still arguing and threatening each other. A lot of words and actions toward her I regret, and I am sure the same is true for her, but she found out I snuck him in, and she was angry with me.

While I was in the hospital, I had to talk about life at home. I told them what I was feeling and going through, and the psychiatrist told me something short and simple: "You are suffering from generational trauma, and you are not the only one with trauma." That made me realize she had her demons too, and people were backlashing her for the 'over-the-top' way she treated me for sneaking out. She cried. It made me feel confused, but then I remembered what the psychiatrist said, and it made me more understanding. Instead of arguing with her about how they were right about how I felt at that moment. I decided to tell her how they were wrong for attacking her, and then our trust and bond got better again over time.

The one thing I was always scared of growing up was being in an abusive relationship. Every woman in my family has gone through it, but I didn't want to. I have already been abused more than once. Do I have to do it again? NO! One very important thing Grandma taught me was, "You bring back to you what you put out to the universe." I am a kind person at heart with no filter and with an attitude only the gods could give; that is exactly how my boyfriend is, which, for me, of course, is perfect. Our relationship is not perfect. We sometimes argue like an old couple, but we laugh after, and I am glad that I took Grandma's words into account. If I would have tried to find someone while I was at my lowest, then they would also be low, and how could they possibly move forward at the speed I was going?

I am now almost 18, an age I thought I would never reach. I am on my course to becoming a veterinarian. I have a dog to call mine, who brightens every part of my day and chews my stuff. I have three of my closest friends to support me when I need to have fresh air outside the house. I have moved forward to the point you would not even know what I have been through. A teacher once told me to write my short-term and long-term goals out on a piece of paper and try to achieve them, even if my short-term goal is getting out of bed and eating. So, I wrote: "1. Ace that test; 2. Make it into an honor roll club." Yes, I did achieve both, and now, my short-term goal is to save for a car, and my long-term goal is to be a veterinarian. I passed my other goals, so what is stopping me from passing these goals? Nothing.

I still fall on my knees sometimes, but I have to keep moving forward. It is the determination and persistence that will make you move. These words make me move: "Hey, you want to go to the pet store?" I will jump out of bed faster than you can blink! It is my special therapy because it makes me happier than ever. Even spiders and snakes make me smile, contrary to most.

My rules: "No one can tell you who you can be" and "Know that your biggest obstacle is yourself." You have your life in the palm of your hands. Why waste it? Forgiveness and self-love are the greatest ways to find success. It is easier for some than others, but it can always be done. You have the power to move mountains, so why are you stuck worrying about that little ant mound?

I still struggle sometimes. I fall like everyone else. It is normal. I still have moments where it is hard to get up, but then, I remember how nice it is to put on fresh clothes and put on or take off my makeup to feel clean. Sometimes it is nice to be that girl in her room binge-watching her favorite shows and eating copious amounts of snacks in her pajamas, but it is also good to feel fresh, loved, and safe. A fresh new start. It was hard to get here, but here I am. Destiny Bogan.

## About Destiny Bogan

 My name is Destiny. Born in St. Charles, MO, in 2005. I am a senior in high school just living life the best anybody could. I work at a local waitressing job and am currently saving for a car and college. My dreams and ambitions all begin with wanting to be a veterinarian, so eight years of college and vet school more or less is mandatory. I currently reside in Florida and am starting my dream life one step at a time with my grandmother and my two little siblings. Being so young, I do not have any special college achievements, but that's just waiting for me in the future. I love music, school, and learning new information on anything like ancient history. I have been through enough you would think I have looked the devil in the eyes and survived. If you asked me today, I would say "Yeah" like it isn't anything to worry about. Only my family and closest friends know my story, but I am here to open my story up for anybody willing to listen or just to know you are not alone. This story is dedicated to my grandma who took me into her loving arms unconditionally when I was four years old and fully when I was 12 and brought me back and showed me the love I needed again to be the person I am today. I also want to thank my beautiful mom and dad who have, through their life lessons, helped me find one of my life lessons.

CHAPTER 11

# In Dedication to My Beloved Wife

Michael L. Sutton

My prayer today and every day is that this book will not only bring enjoyment to its readers, but it will also provide healing for some as it did for me while writing my chapter for it. I pray that it speaks to you.

I remember how our first meeting came about; I had left home as a teenager, wanting more out of life than what I currently had at home. My father was strong-willed; one moment, he went by this set of rules, and the next, there would be another. This didn't sit well with me and was causing friction and confusion in our household between my father and myself, which was hurting the other members of our home and family. So, one day, I decided it was time to leave, and I left, moving three and a half hours away, where there were better work opportunities and less stress.

After a few months away, I began missing my friends and family. And as work started slowing down, it gave me weekends off, allowing me to travel back up north to see them. While there, my buddy and I would get together and head out to the taverns, planning to do some dancing … but there was a drawback. We had to dance with whoever would dance because neither of us had dates. So, one weekend, my buddy mentioned that there was a girl in school whom he'd like to take dancing, but she couldn't go unless she had a friend along. So, I thought about it and said,

"Good deal! You'll get your date, and the friend can be my dance partner." As the next week rolled by, I started becoming anxious; not only to go north once again but also to meet this so-called 'blind date.' All kinds of images and questions rolled through my mind ... What would she look like? Would she be short or tall? What was her name, and who was she? Could she dance? I realize now that this was some pretty shallow thinking, but I wasn't looking for anything long-lasting, just a 'dance partner.' Then, when the weekend rolled around, and I got back up north, I picked up my buddy, and we anxiously drove to meet the girls. I was no stranger to girls or dating, and I had heard of 'blind dates,' but this was to be my first and last.

I will never forget that night. In my eyes, she was beautiful, such a 'looker' standing there in her well-fitting blue jeans and powder blue top, with her long golden hair and big brown eyes. She was a terrific dancer and had a genuine laugh. Not one of giddiness, but of genuine happiness that would not quit. Yet, even with these attributes, there was something else, something strangely different and stronger than anything I had ever felt before. It drew me to her as if by some unknown force. When I looked into her eyes, the glimmer that I could see drew us to each other. That glimmer that I had seen in her eyes then and would see for years to come continued to grab my attention each time our eyes met and continues to touch my heart even now when looking at our old pictures as well as hers.

I grew up in a low- to middle-class family of six, having one brother and two sisters, mom and dad, and I was by no means an 'angel' as they say. For the most part, I remember growing up in our home meant sometimes we were in and church and following strict guidelines, while at other times, not so much. And it seemed to me, as I worked my way through my teenage years, that family and family life were somehow fading, and emptiness, deep loneliness, was continually growing inside of me. I was kind of doing my own thing, but the emptiness was always there and getting harder to ignore.

During those early years, I had some close calls, and I remember my mother being worried about me and asking me numerous times, "You still believe in God, don't you?" And my answer was always the same ... "You know me; I'm always 'hedging my bets'," and I believe that if God is real, then I'm going to heaven; if not, I've got nothing to lose." You see, I had accepted His Son Jesus Christ as my Savior as a youngster, but over the years, I had traveled a lot of distance, and all of it was not on 'good roads.' But God had a way to get me back, and it was through His use of my future wife, whom I had met on that 'blind date'; she was to be the instrument to bring me back into His Fold.

While we were dating, I had agreed to pick my 'yet-to-be' bride up on Sunday mornings and to attend a church near where her family lived. Over time, I watched her walk up to the altar in the church, asking God to be with her. But I stood back in my row of chairs, never walking up with her. I wasn't ready to turn my entire life back over to Him just yet.

After marrying, we continued to go to church, and at one time, we even became custodians of the church we were attending. Throughout our married life, we made it a point to attend church whenever we could. It was important to both of us that after our children were born and grew older, they were in church, learning about God and what He could do for them. In doing so, they both became Christians as well.

Over the years of going to church regularly, I saw how God was blessing us, our family, and our household, but I still resisted. I didn't have a problem with church or living a decent life, but something held me back from giving it my all. However, that was all about to change—and drastically so.

On Thanksgiving night, November 24, 2017, in the early morning hours, I was awakened by the view and feel of my wife leaning over and striking the bed as hard as she could with her fists; she couldn't breathe and couldn't talk. I jumped up, not knowing what was happening in her body or what was causing this, and called for an ambulance immediately.

It seemed like endless hours had passed before the ambulance arrived at our home and the paramedics got to her. I was scared, panicking inside, yet trying to stay calm and reassuring to her, even though by that time, she wouldn't have known. They checked her over quickly, then strapped her onto the gurney, moving her to the ambulance where her heart stopped before leaving our property. The paramedics worked quickly to get it going again and attempted to get her stabilized before and during transport to our local hospital. But just before their arrival, they lost her again. In total, they would lose her five different times before she was well enough to come home, making it the longest 22 days of my life.

I drove to the hospital every day early, to be there as soon as they would let me in ICU, and stayed until I had to leave each night. This made for a lot of hours just watching and waiting, talking to her … but never getting any replies. It gave me a lot of time to think, to reflect on where I was in my life with God. I knew that I had to get myself back to where I needed to be with God before I could ask for any help for my wife, but I had been desperately praying for her just the same.

One night, on my way home, while praying, again, as I was driving, I begged God to give her back to me, to give me more time with her, and—if need be—allow her some of my years if any remained. This was a turning point in my life after all these years; I was finally beginning to understand what genuine love meant and the amount of love God must have had for me to give His Only Begotten Son for me. Right there and then, while driving, I rededicated my life to God and His will. The next morning, as I drove to the hospital, just as I was going through the traffic light in a small town to the south of us, my phone rang. I heard McLaren North, then lost reception, and I panicked; it was too early for them to be on station, I thought. The previous eight days had not been good. Just the day before, the doctors had told me that they had tried everything, and nothing was working to get my wife off the ventilator. I watched them each day trying, and I understood what He was saying. They told me that there was a medicine no longer in use, and if they could find it, they would try it, but if they couldn't, or it didn't work, this morning, it was over.

I pulled off into a market parking lot with my body shaking inside and out, quivering as I had never experienced before, making it impossible for me to keep driving. As soon as I recovered cell service, I called them back, expecting the worse. At that same moment, a song came on the radio, titled "Breathe." Now, this may seem like nothing too many, but I believe in that moment God was telling me to take a breath, and I took a breath, a deep one. The ICU told me that they had been able to get her off the ventilator, and she was doing well. At that very second, on hearing those words, I lost it; the release of all the fear and stress that had built up came rushing out, along with so many sobs and tears of joy.

With surgery and the proper care, my wife's body miraculously began healing. So well that the hospital staff referred to her as a 'miracle.' God graced us with an additional, amazing two-and-a-half years together.

On Friday, April 17, 2020, again, in the early morning hours, something happened. She had suddenly awoken out of her sleep, feeling strange but didn't know why. I checked her vitals and frantically called for the ambulance once again, as her oxygen level had dropped significantly. When they arrived, they brought the gurney right into our home, down the hall to our bedroom, where I had propped her up so she wouldn't fall while I let them in.

Just before their arrival, we had been praying and holding onto each other as tight as possible. I didn't know what was wrong, and I could see the fear in her eyes. I knew that I needed to keep praying and holding on to her. She didn't want me to let go of her, and I didn't want to let go for fear of losing her.

I stood back and let the paramedics work. I had seen enough while they were there and in the past to know that this was not good. Over the next sixteen days, she remained on a ventilator, unaware of anything, while medical professionals worked on her as I, our family, and our church family constantly prayed for her.

Due to the Covid restraints, I was not able to be with her. I tried calling every morning and evening, just desperately wanting to let her know she was not alone, even though they would not let me in. I wanted so much to give her hope, possibly put a spark back in her, to tell her one more time how much I loved her and needed her, but the nurses were always too busy.

One evening, I called and got hold of a nurse who happened to be sitting by her bedside, and he said that he would put the phone's receiver next to her ear and for me to talk. He also said that he didn't know if she would be able to hear me, but I was welcome to talk as long as I wanted. So, I continued just talking to her, telling her everything I needed her to know, with no response. Later, that kind nurse told me he had seen her eyes well up in tears while I was talking to her. This hurt me more than you can ever imagine ... The one I loved and cared so much for was deathly ill, and I couldn't be there for her, talk to her in person, or just hold her. So, I did what I knew to do. I prayed, and I prayed some more; the hardest, most sincere, and loving prayers of my life. I prayed for her healing—and also, if it was not God's will for her to be healed, He take her gently home so she would no longer be needlessly suffering here on earth.

I remembered the fear in her eyes before leaving our home; I told Him I didn't know the plans He had for her, for me, for our family, but I fully trusted Him. He made her and knew what was best for her. He took her home, to heaven ...

We both longed to be together, but it was not to be here again on earth. God answered my prayers and welcomed her home on May 2, 2020.

> "'I wanted somehow to make it not so,' lamented the man, eulogizing a friend who had died young. His words gave poignancy to humanity's ageless heart cry. Death stuns and scars us all. We ache to undo that which cannot be undone."
>
> —*Tim Gustafson*

I did not write *To Lose a Soul Mate* or this chapter with the intention of it being a miraculous cure-all for the immense pain one feels when losing a loved one, a life partner, wife, or husband simply because I don't believe that there is one, aside from God's mercy and time, which doesn't erase the pain but only makes it bearable.

Realizing that death is as much a part of life as living itself is a difficult and emotional concept to deal with. To lose a mate, child, or parent ... to feel the pain and loss that losing someone you love will certainly bring is not something to be taken lightly. Though, as we have seen, and many have experienced throughout the Covid pandemic, it has been even more heartbreaking. To lose someone without being able to see them, hold them, tell them that you love them, or tell them goodbye and not even be allowed to be there as they leave this world for eternity is not something anyone should ever have to endure or be called upon to do. My heart goes out to the many who have had to do just that.

I have no doubt in my mind that had it not been for the love and strength that God, my family, friends, and our church had given to me, the problems that I've faced in just the last few years would have broken me, but they didn't, and they needn't. I'm a survivor. We can all be survivors of a loss such as this. Please don't misunderstand me. I'm not saying we will not have aches and pains both physically and mentally or just days when we're not at the top of our game. Or days when missing loved ones will not feel like our world has just experienced another serious quake. We will, and I do. But we can still wear a smile; though, at times, it may need to be forced through a wall of tears. We can be thankful to be here and be breathing because there are so many who no longer have that opportunity. We are truly blessed to still be alive.

On the days I find it hard to smile, I remind myself of all that God has done for me and our family; to be grateful for every new day, all He has given me, the deep sadness and tragedies He has brought us through. God has given me beautiful memories of those He has chosen to put into my life like my precious wife and my children. I proudly wear a smile whenever possible, even though sometimes it feels like an impenetrable wall of never-ending, sudden grief and tears surrounds me. As I find, the tears I now shed are not all tears of pain or loss but of thankfulness for all that I've been given—God's love, His forgiveness, His connecting my wife's life with mine so many years earlier, the time that He allowed us to be together, His watchful care over my wife while she was in the hospital, and for His taking her home so that she would no longer be suffering here on earth.

The memories God allowed us to make that will carry me through, for our children and our health, and for allowing me to know where she is … and that this is not the end. He has given me hope and an expectation that we will be together again forever in the presence of Christ.

Throughout this stage of my life, I have learned just how little control I have over my life, and that's all right because I know the One who does. My faith in God continues to grow, as I now know that above all else, He has control over my life and the lives of our children, even though they are adults in their own right.

I continue to give thanks often for the family and friends I have been blessed with and for knowing that God has promised us, as followers of Christ, that we *absolutely will* see each other again. This His promise has allowed me to come as far in the healing process as I have.

So, in closing, my friends, if you ever find yourself or someone you care for hurting, needing help or healing, my best advice for you is to simply pray, talking to God as a friend. Give it all to Him. He will hear your pleas for help, as He has heard mine in times of deep sorrow. And He will comfort you, as He has comforted me. Just as He promised, He would.

### Those Who've Gone on Before

*We think of you throughout our days; we long for your presence throughout our nights.*

*We make attempts at staying busy, only to find that nothing can fill the void left by your passing.*

*We try to hide our tears the best way we can so as not to make others relive the hurt we feel each day.*

*When we hear a particular song or see a remembered view, though beautiful, it stirs emotions thought to have been buried.*

*We push back the hurt as we go through birthdays and holidays, knowing in our hearts and minds that you'll not see another.*

*When the days are long, and loneliness tries to take hold, we know that we can take comfort in the memories, words, and love that you have left us.*

*We pray, thanking God for you each day and every night.*

*M.L. Sutton*

## About Michael L. Sutton

 My name is Michael L. Sutton. I was born in Flint, Michigan, and currently live in Cheboygan, which is in northern Michigan. I am a father of two wonderful adult children who also live in Cheboygan. I was married for forty-three years before losing my wife to a health-related illness in May 2020.

I began writing professionally in 2022 with the release of my first book, *To Lose a Soul Mate.* The inspiration for writing this book came after the death of my wife. Writing daily in a journal since her admittance to the hospital as a way to vent the hurt, confusion, and sorrow that her absence was causing me, over time, I noticed that the jumbled words and ill-formed sentences were beginning to take shape and make sense, causing me to feel things I had not felt in my previous writings. When I mentioned this to a friend and showed them my journal, they said that I had a 'gift' and that I should try my hand at writing a book, and that is where it started. Before that, I was enjoying retirement after having worked for 31 years for the State of Michigan Department of Natural Resources as a park manager in various parks throughout the state.

I continue to write for enjoyment—as it gives me a sense of peace and comfort, sharing my material on four social media sites—and as a featured contributor for BIZCATALYST 360° while also working on a second book, which is an anthology or collection of writings from both heart and soul, the yearning and sadness of a broken heart and the gratitude of a thankful and loving heart, fond memories and everyday scenes brought to life, and thought-provoking observations.

It was as if in losing my wife, God had given a gift to me, the gift of writing what my heart felt and my eyes saw as though looking through the windows of my heart.

CHAPTER 12

# The Universe Doesn't Always Accept Your Plans

———

Jean L. Serio CEIC, CPC, CEMA, CSEOP

It was my understanding that the universe provided you with what you needed. However, as I soon discovered, that doesn't mean it brings you exactly what you want, which I came to realize at a very young age. At six, I wanted to become a world-famous ice skater, only to discover classes and coaches were far too costly for a family of modest means such as my own. Not to mention neither of my parents had the time necessary to regularly shuttle me to classes, coaches, and events.

While you rarely see it today, then, big families were the norm. Both my maternal and paternal grandparents had a dozen children each. My father also wanted a large family, which turned out to be six children—three girls and three boys—which meant I was close in age, socialized with, and went to the same Catholic high school as two of my mother's younger sisters. My birthday was just a month apart from her youngest sister's. I loved being with them all. We established excellent relationships, which carried on throughout life, even through marriages and divorce.

Personally, I started my work life very early, far earlier than most. One could say I learned to successfully work in retail at my first non-paying job at age six. Because of the month in which I was born, I would not be allowed to attend school until age seven. So, working with my grandmother was a better option than a babysitter.

Mornings, my mother dropped me off at the local women's dress shop where my grandmother was employed. The owner's children were all in school, and she enjoyed having me around. I was friendly—but not overly so, I was told—helpful, plus came prepared with my books, pencils, and paper to keep me occupied. Grandma brought lunch we shared about noontime on a park bench right outside the store. A space in the backroom was organized where I studied. Now and then, I took a break to fold socks and small items and periodically chat with customers. The owner often said I helped bring in more customers. If this was so, it would be an auspicious start to my first work-life in retail.

Until age eight, my life was that of an average child, but it changed dramatically when my sister (two years younger) was diagnosed with polio—short for poliomyelitis—dubbed Infantile Paralysis. This is a dangerous, contagious, incurable (to date) disease that can paralyze and debilitate in a half dozen ways. A communicable disease that attacks children and requires immunization; in some cases, immunization of those closely associated with the child diagnosed is needed.

While it's been brought to the point of near extinction today, then, children and families were stigmatized; my brother and I were kept separate from our schoolmates; many families with a polio victim were ostracized from society.

That said, after two years of hospitalization, my sister returned home, deemed able to participate in society. My job then became to get her aboard the school bus, walk or ride my bike to school; later, after school, to meet her at the school bus stop (at the corner of our street) and walk her safely the remaining way home. She used crutches then, but when fire drills occurred, I headed to her classroom, picked her up in my arms, and struggled down the stairs (while she carried her crutches) and outside to wait with other students. I repeated this once the drills were over, returning her to the schoolroom. Thankfully, the drills weren't often, and one of the older, bigger kids helped out.

My parents both worked, and I was the one chosen to care for her. And since we were attending the same school, it seemed the best idea at the time. After school, I entertained her by reading, helped her with her schoolwork, took her outside for walks to help strengthen her legs and massaged them as necessary. In short, I did whatever was necessary to help keep her comfortable and learn to talk once again.

While I was helping, in a very important way, it was never easy. I waved back at friends as they walked off together after school to gather at homes to share stories and help each other with homework. Although they often stopped by to visit, eventually, that ended. I continued watching, waving as they strolled by, wishing I could be a part of the group.

Looking back, I realize how stressful it all was—trying to be there for another human being when only a child yourself. I loved my sister and did my best to be there for her—to be optimistic and present, even when I knew my own life was set aside—until far into the future. My parents were both working daily, earning a living to provide us with the best life possible. Who gave me permission to shirk my duties and let others down? Especially my sister who was incapacitated.

Slowly, and with much help, my sister learned to walk. There had been intensive days of workouts and bouts of tears, exhaustive conversations, and enough stress to last a lifetime before she would stand up and on her own. And I remember clearly, it was a day of real celebration for us all! Thankfully, when I headed off to college, she was walking as normally as anyone who had polio could—with a limp. It had taken over a decade. And with it came a variety of added medical issues she endured daily for the rest of her life. Who was I to complain when she had it far worse than I ever would? At that point in life, I thought the universe had finally released me from these heavy responsibilities—it was not meant to be yet.

In my first year of college, my maternal grandfather had a massive heart attack. While he survived, the family was unable to afford private care for him and asked if I would help manage his care at home. The original agreement was, each of my mother's sisters would house him at their homes for four months at a time since they all worked but could organize some time off. Unfortunately, that did not work out, causing issues that prohibited my returning to college quickly. Putting my education on hold—with no possible return in sight—was required.

Eventually, when my grandfather returned to reasonably good health, my maternal grandmother was experiencing her own medical issues. An exhausting time, I juggled back and forth, caring for my sister and grandmother. My job was stretching her legs the way I was shown by her doctor; this was necessary every three hours. I aided her in learning to walk again. Massaging her legs twice a day was also required, plus stretching and massaging her legs during baths. Although stressed out most of the time, I worked diligently at being there for her with high spirits until doctors said I'd done everything that could be done, and my sister needed to begin trying to walk on her own. My mother spent the next six months at home helping her do just that, and I returned to college.

It was discouraging for me. My plan had never been to enter the medical world. Although life seemed to be leading me in that direction, my mind and heart told me I needed something creative I could throw myself into.

Once I returned to school, I applied for a part-time job at a popular boutique in a local mall. It was three nights a week, Saturdays, and an occasional Sunday. It was creative in its own way and thoroughly enjoyable working with customers and having new goals. It was my second exposure to working in retail, and I quickly learned I was good at socializing with and helping customers find what they wanted.

My mother had become pregnant with my younger brother. There had been no issues, so she continued working until she had the baby and returned to work full-time shortly thereafter. One of her sisters, now a nurse, cared for the baby while I continued working with my sister.

I desperately wanted her to get well, praying daily for her good health.

While she eventually learned to walk fairly well, she never walked as most do with a steady stride. That said, I opted not to join college groups and participate in the usual socializing; there simply wasn't enough time. Regardless, it simply wasn't in the cards for me. After all, how much could I do—caring for my sister, working a part-time job, and studying—taking up any other available moments?

I soldiered on but by now was floundering emotionally. While my studies were going well, personally, I had no idea where I was headed. There were many times when I felt I had been deprived of the life I believed I wanted and was angry, with no idea what direction to take to move forward. Why was God or the universe treating me so unfairly?

By the time I graduated, my sister was able to walk relatively well and head off into her own life, having developed a confidence that would lead her forward.

While I may seem ungrateful in my next comment, I do wish I'd had more time for socializing in college. In time, I realized it was a place where lifelong friends can be made. People who may eventually help you secure a job, be there as a shoulder to lean on in difficult times, and also may be emotionally helpful in providing hope and encouragement when you most need it. I'd seen this with others and pined for it now. I needed someone or several who could help me understand my value and maybe even brainstorm with me about what direction to take next.

As crazy as it sounds, I began working at the church bingo on Monday nights at the suggestion of my father. He threw himself into it and made it his life's work to make it fun for all who attended. I met people I'd never known were church members—even saw some relatives and made some new friends. Not only was it fun, but it was also uplifting and turned out to be one of the best things I've ever done. People were chatty and friendly. And the church hall turned out to be the best place to enjoy yourself on a generally quiet Monday night. Plus, you could win money!

For me, another plus was the assistant pastor, Father Hughes, who helped guide me through that emotionally difficult time in my life when I felt lost and disillusioned. While he's long since passed, his valuable words still resonate with me. "Never believe your selflessness deprived you of anything. It was helping provide you with a foundation upon which to better build your life." I made it a point to visit and spend some time with him until he was transferred. There were so many things, about both life and spirituality, he pointed out, which we discussed. Looking back, it was one of the most inspiring points in my life. His simple words of wisdom helped me learn how to manage stress and motivated me to move forward in a more positive way.

I'd worked at the boutique for four years, handled customer situations effectively, taken a class on management, and understood the internal workings of a small retail business. The manager left to pursue another situation, and I was offered her position. I became an excellent salesperson, good at training new hires, and could handle any type of customer situation. And within a year of my promotion, sales had doubled. The promotion was to manage a larger location in a neighboring state.

Before I could make the promotion decision, I ran into my childhood sweetheart at the Monday night church bingo; he was picking up his mother. Later, he dropped her off at home and we went for coffee, spending the next couple of hours chatting about college, our families, and our lives. Turns out he was offered the position of director of the financial department of a well-known corporation. The location was just three miles from the mall in which I'd be working if I accepted the promotion offered me. Since we'd known each other for years, it didn't take long for us to rekindle our romance, accept the promotions offered, and move to our new locations. A year later, we'd married, settled, and bought a home.

In time, my husband's 22-year-old son came to live with us, which presented yet another unique caregiving situation to adjust to and handle. Unsurprisingly, he came with his own issues I then had to deal with.

In time, I discovered I was well suited to becoming an HR pro and moved from management to human resources. And while life brought us a variety of additional, unique issues—health, work, and personal—

to deal with over the years, I realized along the way I had become resilient, determined, and well-organized with the strength to tackle anything which came my way. Eventually, all of this helped me start my own company and thrive.

**In conclusion …**

While my early life, into my late twenties, was difficult and stressful, work and life brought their own unique and difficult issues to deal with, and life seemed to hold me back on a variety of occasions; failure was not an option. While there were many unique situations that presented themselves—too many to present here—the lessons I've learned when life pushed me to the brink of failure prepared me well for a successful future, job situations, and marriage. Also, it's important to remember failure can help us develop the strength to tackle tough times when they arise.

That said, my favorite quote is from Winston Churchill: "Success is not final; failure not fatal. It is the courage to continue that counts."

## About Jean L. Serio CEIC, CPC, CEMA, CSEOP

Jean is a certified employment interview coach, a recognized LinkedIn and resume expert, a story-tell interview coach, a certified personal branding coach, and a freelance coach. She has developed six job training programs.

She has been a guest on Solo Pro Radio, LinkedIn Summit—one of 200 top LinkedIn experts, 2016—and various podcasts. She is a featured contributor on:

- BizCatalyst360
- Business.com
- LinkedIn News
- BLR-Daily HR Advisor
- ERE's Daily HR Advisor
- RecruitCon
- Next Ave. div of PBS
- Job Conference International
- beBee International
- Medium
- Entrepreneur HQ Magazine
- Self Growth
- Forbes

Released February 2023 -

*Is it Time for a Career Reinvention or a Career Pivot?*

# CHAPTER 13

# Peace in the Mirror

—

## Curtis Gregor

I can look in the mirror. It does not sound like much, but I can look in the mirror with peace and contentment. I struggled to look in the mirror most of my life. I was ashamed of what I saw. I was embarrassed by the physical look on my face. I was never encouraged for what I could do. I never felt good enough.

I grew up on a small ranch in rural North Dakota. The nearest 'town' had a post office/grocery/gas pump store, a saloon (only served beer), a grade school (one teacher, one room, about 7 students on average), and our church. We attended church every Sunday. It was not our school district.

I started school in the town a little farther away in the other direction. It had a grade school. Three grades when I started. I was in the last class that attended that school. Main Street had a bar, a post office, and a general store. The general store had two aisles. Clothes and notions in one aisle, and groceries in the other one. In the fall, they would get in one fifty-five-gallon barrel of Lutefisk that would sit on the porch. Grandpa would always buy enough Lutefisk for a nice meal for everyone. The meal was always Lutefisk, homegrown mashed potatoes, homegrown and canned sweet corn, and melted butter.

What is my story? I usually do not speak about my story. I will sometimes speak out small parts that relate to what someone is struggling with. I will start with the last major story that changed my life one more time.

A little over three years ago, I woke up at 5:30 a.m. on a Saturday morning with a nosebleed that would not stop. I waited until my girlfriend woke up in her bedroom after 7:00 a.m. and called the nurse helpline. They recommended that I go to the emergency room. After about two hours, they got the nosebleed to stop. The doctor told me that he could put me in the hospital. I did not believe him. He said "Yes" and left to get a second opinion. I was extremely lucky in that the doctor that came in had semi-retired, moved to the area, and only worked in the hospital. He had a lot of experience with high blood pressure. I spent two days in a cardiac critical care unit for a nosebleed. Yes, a nosebleed. After two days of headaches caused by Nitro drips and a handful of prescriptions, I left the hospital. I stopped sleeping with my wonderful girlfriend Val. I have never told her why. Her first knowledge of what I experienced will be when she proofreads this for me.

I had violent nightmares often. For about two years, I wondered two to four nights a week if I would wake up. I did not want her to wake up next to my dead body. She had to bury her daughter, and soon after, her stepfather, and then her daughter's long-term boyfriend. Her stepfather had been an important figure in her life since she was a little girl. She also watched as several of our separate friends were laid to rest in the last few years.

I had follow-up visits with both a primary care physician and a cardiologist. I talked to them both about the side effects of the drugs. They cause me to be weak, take naps every day, have headaches, and cause me to have a difficult time completing my thoughts. I was so weak that I often had to stop when walking from the car to the apartment. I would collapse on the bed and nap after a trip up the stairs. Some days, I refused to drive. I avoided people on the worse days. Before writing this, I only talked to about fifteen people about what I had experienced. During the follow-up visits, the doctors both said that there is nothing else to do. The cardiologist said that many people take one medicine for high blood pressure. Some people take two medicines for it. I take five. I take seven pills a day. Both doctors said in plain English, "Take the medicine or die."

As I said, I grew up on a small ranch in rural North Dakota. I am the middle child of three. I have an older brother and a younger sister. I am of German and Norwegian heritage. I grew up in a culture where the oldest male gets everything. A young girl is always the baby and treated special.

I grew up a one-half mile from my paternal grandparents and uncle. It was three miles by road, two miles across the shortcut trail, or a one-half mile across through the wet pasture. When I was about 10 years old, my father started a new trail that cut the travel down to a mile. We were there at least once a week. They were a major part of my formative years.

In March 1977, my parents left without saying anything. We were just home from the nearly hour-long school bus ride. They did not come back for a long time. When they finally did return, we found out that grandpa had gone out to feed the calves in the cold. He was 80 years old. He had to crawl up into the hay rack to fork the feed around. He had a heart attack. I heard the coroner say they did not believe he felt the hay when he fell into it.

January 1st, 1978; it was freezing cold, about 20 degrees below zero Fahrenheit. We had Sunday lunch with my grandmother and uncle as was normal. My uncle went out to do his afternoon chores before he left for Fargo to visit someone. He never came back. He had a farm accident 100 feet from where my grandfather died. This was a really impactful change in my life. Someone stayed with Grandma, and usually, it was Mom for a while. Mom had always been there in the morning and at night before.

Grandma found out she had cancer in her stomach in the spring. She had major surgery and many heavy treatments of chemo. She was tired and sick until the next fall when she passed away. Yes, that was three people gone from the immediate family in three years. Nothing was close to the same in my life after that.

After a very tough time, things seemed to be calming down. I can tell you what I was doing at 6 a.m. March 12$^{th}$, a year after the passing of my grandmother. It has been a few years. I was playing two-handed Pinochle with my dad. We had been playing for quite a while by then. I had woken up extra early; I went upstairs through the dark utility space and stairway. The bedroom was added when my sister came. The lights were never updated to turn on lights on the stairway from the bottom. Yep, I grew up feeling my way up or down in the dark.

I remember getting ready for school. When I was done, Dad had left to start chores for the day. Livestock always needs attention. I never saw my father again. That night, after school, he had not returned from finishing chores. He was found dead in a building with a tractor he was working on. Four in four years.

I was born with a slight physical defect. When I was a teenager, I received braces. It was a huge expense for a family with a small ranch. The braces required missing school every month for part of one day. It was a sixty-mile drive to an orthodontist at the time. The braces were combined with jaw surgery. My jaw had been half an inch short all my life. I seldom talked to people and did not want to be noticed because I always felt stared at. The surgery lengthened my jaw. The braces did straighten and partially align my teeth. Part of the surgery was to cut the muscle under my jaw. I have had a double chin ever since. To someone who has always been a little heavy, it was horrible the first time I saw it. I sometimes still do not like to be seen or speak in front of people. I avoid pictures, and I never use a full tooth smile.

I was never encouraged to be a 'real person.' I was told to do things but never told that I could do anything well. I remember doing chores on the farm as soon as I started school. I was responsible for feeding and watering the chickens. I remember not being strong enough to lift the five-gallon bucket of feed. I had to make two trips for a long time with a three-gallon bucket. Chickens need feed and water every day, snow or not. Eggs need to be picked when they are fresh. The winters in North

Dakota can bring snowbanks reaching 10 feet high in the yard. The temperatures vary from 100 degrees Fahrenheit to 30 degrees below zero. I had other chores as well.

I remember being in the barn while my mom milked the six to eight cows by hand. The milk was used in the house. My favorite food is sour-cream spice cake. The cream was put in cans and sold in town with the eggs for grocery money. The milk that the cream was separated from was fed to the pigs. Dad had pigs until they stopped milking cows when I was about five years old. Mom says I was there twice a day, even while I was still in diapers. It was a ranch, and everyone worked to make it succeed. Kids had to sit and watch or help. There were no babysitters.

I remember that something happened between my father and my uncle. They quit farming together when I was just out of the first grade. Until then, I spent many days riding a B International tractor with my grandfather. The tractor had the seat on the right side and a wooden toolbox with a lid on the left side. When I was old enough, I got to ride on the toolbox and hang on. Occasionally, grandpa would let me dump the rake. I soon was raking on my own.

Dad stood on the tractor and pushed in the clutch. He said, "If anything goes wrong, push this switch down." He placed the tractor in first gear, set the throttle, let out the clutch, and stepped down to the ground. He walked around the right end of the 14-foot international dump rake while I was raking scatterings—up and down each windrow, overlapping in the middle, and filling the rake before dumping. Oh, yeah, do not hit the fences! When the rake was full, I leaned back as far as possible, reached back with both hands, and jerked as hard as I could. That was the only way I could dump the rake. I raked hay every summer until I graduated from high school. Raking got easier as I grew.

The next year, my uncle built two 32 ft. dump rakes from old rakes and 1950 Chevrolet car front brakes and master cylinders. I learned how to drive straight, turn short corners, have patience, take pride in my work, and put in long hours. Raking gave me a lot of time to think after I learned how to do a good job. I have no idea how many miles I drove or thousands of acres I have raked.

I recall a retired pastor talking about a generation of people that did not need to be entertained disappearing. He was talking about my father's generation. He was speaking in a rural church that was mostly farmers and ranchers. He still delivers a message every week. I was a throwback to this generation. I still almost never have the radio on in a car or tractor when I am in them and hardly ever watch TV. My mind is always thinking about a problem or several. I am a lifelong problem solver with professional training in both the diesel mechanics and business fields.

I did not understand the value of *me* or what I could do until a few years ago. I was never good enough, picked for things, or celebrated. I thought that money, position, and title meant that people were smarter and better than me. They could not be wrong by what I was told my whole life. Unlike most people, I can point to the day and the incident that changed my life. About seven years ago, the company I was employed by participated in a fundraising event for a large non-profit group. The company talked about safety every day. The top people regularly stood up front at meetings, talking about following safety policies and being safe. They talked about how safe the company was to work at. I worked the second shift from 4:30 p.m. to 2 a.m. One night, at about 10 p.m., they were having a pot-luck event. The second-highest person in the company was preparing a seafood broil for the employees to try. He was outside by another event when I came out to watch for a few minutes before we ate. He was standing next to a turkey fryer filled with boiling water and the food he was preparing. He was standing there in his bare feet and sandals. This was a company that required steel-toed shoes in most of the building just to be there.

I waited until no one was close and quietly spoke to him about the dangerous situation and his example. He promptly told me to mind my own business. Something snapped in my mind as I walked away. My mind repeatedly played what I had seen and his response. I realized that I was right. I also realized that what I had been seeing for years was accurate. I had always been awed by other people and led to believe they are better than me. I woke up the next day with my life changed. I reviewed a lot of my life. I saw where what I had predicted often to myself had come true. Each day since then, I have become more powerful in what I can do.

About 12 years ago, a young lady with physical and developmental challenges came into my life with her brother that also had developmental challenges. She spent many of the first months of her life in the intensive care unit. She had several open-heart surgeries before I met her. She was very intelligent and possibly the greatest example of a 'Christian' I have ever seen. She used her very limited income to make Christmas presents for the 20 people she gave them to every year. For years, she referred to me as her father. I helped carry her to her last resting place about four years ago; she was only 33. I had many talks with her about peace and her value. I was one of the few people that treated her as a person with value and not someone challenged by life circumstances. She spent most of the years I knew her terrified of dying. She said she trusted me. In the last months, she never talked about being terrified of dying.

Six years ago, I did the unthinkable. I walked away from a job with no idea where I was going. The environment was very negative, and regardless of what management said, the 'Good Old Boys Club' was much more important than written company policy. I chose to walk away with no idea of a paycheck. I do not recommend this approach. Somehow, the bills have always gotten paid. I returned to technical college for a business degree to get a better job. It was the first thing I did after walking away from the last toxic environment.

One young lady, who was very quiet, sat near me in several classes. I noticed she had low self-esteem, but she was always friendly to me. After a few days, I was inspired to try to help her. I slowly started to encourage her to feel better about herself. She soon became more confident and was an excellent student. She graduated and moved out of the area a happier young lady.

I have taught a couple of groups of people how to see things differently. The results have been amazing for some. One group was the Minnesota Community College Moorhead Student Government when I was president for one semester. The policy was that the members of the board could keep their positions if they liked. The track record was that almost all representatives quit at the end of the semester. Four of us decided to stay for the next semester. Because we were the only ones returning, we were the board. I asked for the presidency based on my desire to teach true leadership. I prepared and inspired others to recruit people for the rest of the student government positions. We needed 12 more. Two weeks after the spring semester started, we had the first student government election that anyone at the college could remember. Some of the staff had been there for 20 years. That does not prove anything about me as a leader. A leader is someone who makes a difference after they leave. When I graduated, everyone that was still going to be in that college was planning to come back to student government. That change is a sign of leadership. I did it by changing what people saw. They then changed how they thought and what they did.

I have made many decisions that I would not make with the information I now have. I have been married and divorced twice. I paid a high price for those decisions. Worse than what I have experienced, my children are paying a price for those decisions as well. What my children had to experience is the most difficult thing that I must live with.

A long time ago, I saw and experienced a lot of pain. I have long believed that there must be a purpose for or from our experiences. I have been motivated by the pain of my past to help others feel better about themselves. Only through first believing in ourselves can we grow.

I spent much of the past fifteen years helping someone couch surfing with a drug addiction understand their value. He now has a construction job, a driver's license, and a checking account and is trying to help others.

I was placed in a position to complete a project with a young lady who didn't see her value. She is a National Honor Society member. Her greatest regret while getting her college degree was getting one B grade. We worked together for three months because she made several previous attempts at suicide. She even made one while we were working together. I was able to help her in a few short discussions to see her value. She now has been married for two years and is hoping to have a child. When I showed up to read at her wedding, her father asked me why I traveled two hours to read at her wedding. I said, "Because she is special." I will remember the look on his face for a long time.

I live each day to not have regrets tomorrow. I can forgive myself for the poor choices that I made with the information that I had at the time. I live for a more positive life each day.

*My story has many more parts.*

*I still help people see their value in many ways.*

*My story grows each day.*

*My power grows each day.*

*I desire to have people not struggle as I have.*

*We each are critical to the world with the talents we are born with.*

*I look in the mirror now in peace.*

## About Curtis Gregor

A small physical defect marked his life forever. The shortened jaw left scars long beyond the surgery that corrected it. People that are looking at him make him feel like they are staring at his defect.

He has spoken in front of thousands of people. He has overcome his feeling of inferiority by understanding that his knowledge and perspective are valuable to others. He now spends his time troubleshooting problems across a long range of subjects. He understands that successful solutions come from understanding the system and what is out of place. He successfully helps individuals one at a time and is working on expanding this process to groups of people.

Curtis has successfully helped people learn how to appreciate the value of their talents in the big picture. He works to promote individuals in their own minds. Curtis has successfully turned around attendance and engagement in groups.

Curtis and his girlfriend Val turned around the attendance at Red River Singles club in a few short months. They focused on marketing, attendees' desires, and customer service. They raised the attendance from about thirty per dance to nearly one hundred. Curtis can feel and label the parts of a situation that do not feel right.

Curtis has written an unpublished 7,000-word pamphlet on the path he traveled. He suggests to those that are struggling to find themselves. He strongly believes that every individual has talents. The talents of everyone are necessary to the whole of society. His dream is to help people continue to raise others' self-esteem.

# CHAPTER 14

# Not a Victim

---

## Johanna Baker

If we were friends, I loved having you over to dinner. Entertaining was an opportunity to meet and talk with people and get to know them better. This was true for many years in my early married life. Then it came to a halt.

Let me tell you a little about my background. After WWII, my parents immigrated to the US, and at the time, I was but an infant. My parents were displaced persons, fleeing into Austria with what they could carry. What my mother described was getting into freight trains like you saw in the Dr. Zhivago movie, where people were squeezed tightly in a box car, fleeing for their lives with the clothes on their backs and mementos that fit in small bags. She told me they buried any valuables they had in their backyard. Little did they know they would never return.

My parents met each other in Austria, fell in love, and married. If you haven't seen the beauty of the Austrian Alps, look them up; this is where I was born, between where two rivers converged. To this day, it's still remote, where people go white river rafting. They decided they would immigrate to America for more opportunities. They came over from Hannover, Germany, with an American military ship—the SS Sturgis. They came through New Orleans on their way to Los Angeles in January, where it was cold and raining cats and dogs.

My mom cleaned office buildings and toilets after they arrived here. My dad, who was a forestry engineer, built picnic tables and worked for the city, lifting manhole covers. My dad went back to school as soon as he could to become a civil engineer. They were very industrious but, as immigrants often do, started out at the bottom living in a garage and worked themselves up from there.

My life growing up was a fairly happy childhood recognizing the times my parents had—where there was no work, and we went through difficult financial periods. The expectation my parents had of my siblings and me was to do well in school. Expectations were set at a high bar for all of us. I was the oldest of three.

As I grew older, I remember asking my mom lots of questions about what happened during WWII. She was in Castle Germany when it was firebombed. She was about 20. She was very frightened of Hitler and the SS. Anyone who said anything negative about the Hitler regime was subject to being taken away. She tried to mind her Ps and Qs. She was supposed to visit friends the night of the firebombing, and she had an intuition that she should not go. She always felt she was somehow spared to do something with her life. The horrors of war and all she lived through made a huge impact on me. So much suffering, so much death. I began to have a deep respect for what my parents lived through and how they survived. The people in Europe during the Second World War endured much suffering and death. I think it made me tougher when there were difficulties I bumped up against growing up. My view of the war from the American perspective was much less graphic of what really happened.

After attending UC Berkeley during the tumultuous years of the Vietnam war when most students were protesting because our fellow students were coming home in body bags, I ended up having a falling out with my father who had taken a very authoritarian view of anyone protesting what the government was doing. I ended up moving in with my future husband Jim, who has been the love of my life. Living together before marriage was not as accepted then as it is now. We married a year later and have been married for over 50 years.

We waited seven years before deciding to have children. We wanted to be more stable before taking on the responsibilities of raising children. During the early years of our marriage and after having our first daughter Erika, we got involved with a group called 'Beyond War.' Nuclear proliferation was in full swing at that time. This buildup of nuclear weapons at that time was horrendous; we could end all life on the planet if these were used. Because of my mother's experience with war, it became very personal to me that we didn't want to blow ourselves up. We did home meetings, explaining the problem of the many bombs. We would use a coffee can partially filled with bee-bees from a bee-bee gun, pouring it into another can to hear how senseless so many bombs would be. How many times do you want to blow up the planet?

After my first daughter was born, I lost sight in my right eye. I saw an ophthalmologist who thought this was due to birth control pills. Of course, I stopped taking them. My sight came back after about six weeks, and life continued. Going to work, caring for our baby, and running a household; it was hectic.

After about four years of working, I ended up in a very stressful job. I started having a very hard time with my job. Jim and I decided we would expand our family, and I got pregnant again. I found I couldn't walk very quickly, which made my little Napoleon complex boss crazy. I worked in Silicon Valley, manufacturing electronics components for the electronics industry. I worked in the materials side, planning and coordinating with the manufacturing line and QA to get things out on time. My boss liked to create a fire and then come in to be the hero to put the fire out. That meant quality control and test put in 12 to 14 hours a day to meet his schedule. I was put in a real squeeze because my training was to make the materials ordered get to the manufacturing floor on time so that things would run smoothly. He made the entire plant jump through hoops to meet deadlines. He got fired after I was gone because he cost the company so much money. I worked in what is now called Supply Chain Management.

After that tormenting time in that stressful job, I finally left that job and came home, now pregnant with Kathleen. My physical difficulties kept getting worse. The stress I had been under did take its toll. I kept falling. During this time when I was having so much trouble physically, I was introduced to a book that changed my life. I read Viktor Frankl's *A Man's Search for Meaning*. This book has been transformative for me.

After Kathleen was born, things got worse for me physically. I now believe it was the hormone changes that happen in a woman's body after pregnancy. It was three years of problems, starting to cook at 2 p.m. and not being able to put dinner on the table till after 7. Everything was like pulling my body through a snowstorm. Everything was hard for me. When I couldn't get up from a chair, my husband insisted I find out what was going on with me.

At that time, I thought I needed to do my exercises better and do different exercises than I had been doing. I was told I needed to see a neurologist. My doctor did many, many tests and finally did a definitive spinal tap. He walked into my hospital room very matter-of-factly and told me that I had multiple sclerosis. This was in 1986. I didn't even know what that meant. It's like having a telephone system, and the message never gets to the muscle. I was soon to find out what it might mean. He told me I needed to put bars on all the walls and to be prepared to be in a wheelchair for the rest of my life. I was 35 years old, just when I was able to really go after what I wanted to do.

I must explain the fundamental shift that happened to me after reading Dr. Viktor Frankl's book, *Man's Search for Meaning*. Dr. Victor Frankl was a psychotherapist and was put into a Nazi concentration camp during WWII. He came out of this experience transformed. Here are the fundamentals of what he learned: Everyone can go through hardships. None of us is immune. Our only choice is how we respond to what happens to us. What is our attitude when everything is taken away from us? Our only response is to be responsible and develop a positive attitude about it. We are born with a mission or purpose to fulfill. How can we give of ourselves to the world?

To summarize, Victor Frankl said that we can have everything taken from us, but what we have a choice about is our attitude toward it. He came out of the concentration camp after all of his family was killed. He was starved. He saw incredible suffering and death. He saw people marched to the incineration chambers. How we perceive what is happening to us is critical. I was not going to be a victim of this diagnosis. Dr. Frankl came out transformed after his experience in the concentration camp. I was determined to transform myself.

He said that man needs to have a potential struggle to be who we are and who we become. We want to be in the now, to move in the direction of joy and happiness—not to pursue but ensure it—because we must commit to something bigger than ourselves to give our lives more meaning.

What did that mean to me? I was not going to let a diagnosis define me. Some things are invisible to others like PTSD, depression, mental illness, chronic fatigue, and even cancer, and others are so visible they can't be ignored. I was aware that what happened to me was visible, and I needed to rise above it.

Raising my two beautiful daughters has helped me gain purpose to help and guide them to become independent women who can take care of themselves. I am so very proud of both of them.

In 1988, I went to Germany for a treatment that worked for me. I went from not walking when I entered the hospital to walking with a cane when I got home 11 days later. Using the cane continued for a long time. Sometimes it was a symbol to not bump into me. The support of my family was also critical in helping me feel I was worth saving.

Supplemental nutrition improved the quality of my life and my functioning. I have continued that journey to help myself. All the people I met when I was first diagnosed have all passed. They went down the traditional medical route. Do remember, there were no treatments in the 1980s but cortisone. I did try a couple of the new treatments that are available now and developed a bleeding ulcer. My doctor, who gave me a blood transfusion, said that my reaction was due to my immune system being compromised. I made the decision I would fight this to stay functioning as much as I could. Here we are, 35 years later, and I am still here.

After rotator cuff surgery, I now need to use an electric wheelchair. I am now helping others get healthier and feel better. My purpose is to help others in any way I can.

I have found, with our foods no longer having all the nutrients in them that they had before WWII, and our soils overworked without rejuvenation, we need to supplement with great supplemental nutritional products to help us stay as healthy as possible. I am here to help others in any way I can with what I've learned.

As I told you previously, I loved to entertain and found text, zoom, and social media to have meaningful connections to make my life more meaningful. We deserve to stay strong, even when faced with many difficulties. We need to believe in ourselves that we are more than what has happened to us. Remember, if Dr. Viktor Frankl could live through, come out of his experience, and find his way back to life, we can too. He has given us tools to help us survive many difficulties and find meaning in what we are going through. I wish for you hope and grit to survive whatever life has thrown at you.

Look for and live for all the happy moments you can, for you are worth it. I have been able to find joy, and I pray you find happiness and joy in all the small, beautiful moments that our creator has provided for us. Nature is very healing. Gratitude for all we've been given can give us peace and appreciation for all the sentient animals, people, plants, and flowers that grow and help us realize that we, too, are a part of this unique life plan to live and thrive. You are a part of this beautiful life and deserve to be filled with joy!

## About Johanna Baker

Johanna Baker is a wife, mother, and grandmother. She grew up in Fullerton, California, in a home of first-generation immigrants to the United States. Her first language was German, and she learned English playing with the neighborhood children when she started kindergarten.

She thrived in the public school system, and in high school, she loved being a part of theater, many musicals, and plays. She went off to college during tumultuous protests in the Vietnam war. Attending the University of California at Berkeley at that time heightened her awareness that the war should end.

After college, Johanna worked in supply chain management in Silicon Valley. Following her diagnosis of multiple sclerosis, she subsequently continued her effort toward making a recovery. She started her own business with a partner videoing the 1906 earthquake survivors. She later continued as an entrepreneur helping teams of people with their health issues and working with people to develop leadership skills.

She is grateful for being able to continue contributing to the personal growth of others.

CHAPTER 15

# Soul Songlines

———

## Kathleen Dutton

*Why Soul Songlines*? Kathleen spent time in Australia and was taken with primordial nature of Aboriginal song. Her writing engages the conditions of life and the eco of a place to belong in the same way as the present-day indigenous Australians, while appreciating the ancient art and culture of the people and language that is symbolic of what connects us all, from ancient Chinese characters to the narrative of the Songlines are the touchstone of the creation stories. The sketchbook chronicles her travels through the places of her origin and her observation and various encounters, while within the text is little meditation ideas and musings on the nature of what it is to be a human, a soul.

*Proust: more perspicaciously than any other writer, reminds us that the 'walks' of childhood form the raw material of our intelligence.*

*Bruce Chatwin, The Songlines*

## Walking with the Divine in London & Essex

There was an understanding that it was not possible to continue. It was crumbling. The drama is always accurate, pointing us in the direction of what is wanted. The story, now already past. A 'healing pause' was essential to recalibrate a new life unfolding. Yet, at times, lost, angry, frustrated, and scared; infinitely better for stripping away what was unwanted. Suddenly, I was thrown into nowhere land. One bag and me!

So, each day, I practiced qigong, Raja meditation, prayer, and walking the land of my birth. With the help of my sister and friends, I moved a few things and put them into storage in Essex. It was the beginning of a healing journey of hope, joy, and faith.

I've included the extracts from my diary, which I entered on my iPhone and in sketchbooks at that time of the first few days. I write words and image stories, as these express what I learned more authentically.

Einstein said, "Everything is energy and that's all there is to it. Match the frequency of the reality you want and you cannot help but get that reality."

*"What's the story? Why is the story important for me to tell at this time?" When recently asked to write a story about hope, to communicate the catalyst for change in my life, it was a challenge. Without going into all the blame narratives, indeed I felt a block. Then a realization that the stories about our life become our lives, aware it also shapes how we live to some extent. Do I create hell or paradise? In each moment, choosing peace within. The thing*

*is how to stay in that frequency, even in challenging circumstances. At that time, spending time alone, there's great power: in walks each day, drawings, and deep soul whispers. In truth, I found myself creating something precious out of nothing.*

*Do I take you back to a moment? Due to the end of what was a long period of being in conflict with one soul of over 20 years, it reached a point where I couldn't stay, and the dynamic had become toxic. What was 'love' was broken—and me too. Yet, at that time, there was an awakening. It was a painful experience. I also hurt my back and was pushed into a re-evaluation of everything, even the things I liked about my life changed forever—my home, friends, and work. It was like at the same time I was guided softly and saw the divine in all things. Everyone's a gift. At the same time as huge waves of sadness, grief, and fear. I'm sharing these few days. I walked ... I walked and walked.*

## Sunday Evening 8th March 2020

Walking started at Willesden through to Willesden Green and onto Cricklewood. I noticed the moon—almost full; the light of the streets. There are cozy cafes and new walls painted on the road, welcoming people to Willesden Green. My favorite colors are turquoise and bright pastels on the wall.

The faces of those around me look amazing, each a unique divine expression of God. After attending **International Women's Day** this evening and meeting with many like-minded souls and meditation, my energy is high. I feel full of love. I smile at others, and they smile back.

Life is so simple ... life in this moment full of the stories of the day and the peaceful energies of my soul and connecting to all souls at the spiritual university today.

I feel peace and kindness in my own heart and see kindness in the eyes of those around me, and the peace in me spills over into these streets. The darkness of the night feels cool on my skin. I'm aware the pain in my back has subsided.

**Monday 9th March**

Cricklewood to Willesden Green in Northwest London. I awake and do ... meditation at 4.44. I look up the meaning on google ... **MESSAGE from ANGELS.**

*444 is a number of protection and encouragement. It is a sign that you are currently following the right path. If you see the number 444 repeatedly, it is often your angel giving you a sign that they are with you. The sign is reminding you to feel confident and supported in this knowledge.* I spent time healing myself, had acupuncture and did qigong, and I ran groups in London down by the river and in Willesden Green for myself and Earth.

Thinking about what this time in London has been like for me, the roles do not define this being. Who am I, then? I am a soul in roles: mother, artist, designer, and healer. The awareness that my personality is not me either; of course, it's part of me. How do I bridge conscious awareness and the everyday? I love art and healing. How do I bring these together? The place RSL Collective on a Tuesday; our 'Angel Day' with my friend Loretta worked together, meeting lots of different healers at that time, also doing an exchange of services from Vortex Healing, Angelic Hands on Healing, and Theta Healing with Katy Sophia at her company Soul Radiance.

I've always had lucid dreams and used them for my work as a creative director and artist. However, now, I started to dream of healing circles with women: inner child, healing the mother wound, and Tibetan healing circles. With a little bit of help from my friends, we set them up as one-off events in both the Southbank, London, by the River Thames and in Northwest London, connecting with other circles and groups too after dreams of a Circle of Global light, this one with Mikhail Multidimensional Healing, and we found others to join. I'm uplifted by all souls working to heal both their self and the earth through our connection to divine love. In fact, for me, the combination of acupuncture, qigong, and meditation brings physical and spiritual healing together and works well.

*I feel well. The walk today; my eyes see other souls rushing by ... trees ancient on the road. They have seen lifetimes ...The clouds shift across the sky between buildings, and I notice a small flower in the crack of the road. A bluebell.*

*There are sprouting optimistic daffodils in gardens, bright against the gray of the streets here ...*

*The pink blossoms on trees really caught my eye today. They speak my heart of pure love ... pink heart energy blooming throughout the street. Potential energy; nature's resilience. The color of love.*

The inner being that connects us all to that 'Big love,' plus peace, purity with great strength, allows us to step into a new way of being responsible for our own response to what is ... be that family, friends, or the news. It gets my attention on the soul stirs; it's time to discern where the soul's life force is going.

*Today, taking a moment to consider. What am I choosing to feed? Find the way to direct your soul's energies to love and healing. It's like that movie "The Hunter" with Robert Mitchum: Cut to scene with one hand; 'love' and 'hate.' Seeing that duality. Aware of a new cycle beginning ... Huge step. Realize the real lies and illusion that I've sat within ... in silence and draw.*

*Fear is taking my energy: False Evidence Appearing Real ... It happens. I see it when a wave hits me. Learning to let it flow through ... lots of healing tears. I listen to guided meditation before sleep: Louise Hay's "You can heal Yourself."*

**Tuesday, March 10 (My birthday)**

*Today, as the sun rises (6 a.m.): Meditation.*

*6.30 a.m.: Healing Group Soul Earth Ancestors.*

*7 a.m.: Forgiveness is our focus today.*

*Conscious that where energy flows, it grows ... Awareness of how I live each day, attention to the values of soul: love, peace, purity. Through the ripples of this energy we each fuel the world.*

*1 p.m.: South Kensington this day. Walk where I used to live as a small child till around six to seven years old. Indeed, memories of happy days; nice times with my mum and dad, brother, and extended family.*

*Today, College of Psychic Studies: Angel Healing ... I ascend up 111 steps all clean, the door heavy. The building is the same as the one I lived in with my family as a child. The basement, doors, windows, and stairs are all the same as in our home many moons ago.*

On the street, there are 'constant things,' stuff that has stayed the same: the station, streets, one shop. The buildings are all white Georgian style with pillars at the entrance that look into a square. The trees are probably the oldest thing on the roads here and have seen it all evolving. The cobblestones of the mews: a friendly reminder of how time changes things; we no longer have horse-drawn carriages. Yet they are here ... shall I focus on the past I know and see or the emerging way that is unknown? Feeling like an un-carved block or a blank page in my sketchbook ready to be created. Today, taking this moment to consider, "Shall I focus on what is working out for me, rather than against my new path?" I waver.

**Wednesday, March 11**

*After morning meditation at 5.55 a.m.*

*Healing with group self and Earth.*

*Stayed in Ilford -Trip to Lea on sea walk along the coast. Much appreciation of light beauty, contrasting light over the sea, high tide. Flow and stillness.*

*Joy within this walk with another beautiful soul by my side. I encounter other friendly happy souls. Vegan food and so much peace. A stop at a cafe with love notes from angels in the interior. There is much love here. There are celestial skies; the sun beams with radiant lines of light that illuminate the sea and sky, and then they are gone. I'm really amazed at this beautiful coastline. There is a pink bobble hat on a seat that has been left behind by a child. It looks as though it is waiting to be found.*

*Yachts moored up on land, fishing boats large and small bobbing out at sea. The smell of the sea and coffee drift past my nose. There is the sound of waves sloshing against the sides of boats, and gulls screech into the blustery sky.*

*Love this moment.*

*"We are one love" sings in my heart.*

## Thursday, March 12th

*Today, the soul asks in a whisper, "Can you be very present in this moment in nature? Listen with your heart?"*

## Ilford - South Park, Essex

What a few days ... this time, another place I lived with my family in this life when I was a teenager and visited in my 20s. All different in the town, yet this park has that constant holding of space through nature, the trees, little lake, and stream.

Grounding the light within the healing group Multidimensional Healing and also with dear soul and friend in Essex who also sees what we feed and focus on helps those energies grow.

*Today, I truly feel that need to be magic. So I actually created a circle healing round park, going from tree to tree, walking. Their ancient roots are so far below the drama ... Above all, it is a time to act with courage.*

*Feed love.*

*Not fear.*

*Went from London to the Essex countryside.*

*From River Roding to the sea.*

*Grounding meditation outside. Divine creator of all that is … I am peace. Healing the highest good my soul, ancestors, and … Earth and out into the universe.*

*Healing walk that brings me back into my body and presence.*

## Friday 13 March

After morning meditation at 5.55 a.m. Healing with a group online for self and Earth. 11 a.m., my mind flashes for a moment to some of the art created in 2012. An exhibition on the Southbank, London, "Everything is Energy," exploring the earth's Schumann resonance and our interconnection as humans. I was thinking about that and turned on my phone, and there was a talk by Matt Khan, saying, "Everything is here to help you."

My body feels happy and full of energy … appreciation that now, this time, I'm with my parents. I appreciate time with family and friends.

Appreciate all that is in nature. Appreciate our city's dynamics and the peace in the rural areas on both land and sea.

Yes, life is forcing us all to be still and rest and be. It is part of the clearing release. Honoring the process. Listening.

All about simplifying. Sometimes that ego chat creates a wave of thinking, *What if this and that …?* More drama, more complicated twists and turns. I stop; it passes.

Now, I have not been looking at this in the media. I don't read or listen to the news, but still, I pick things up. A friend of mine said, "Everyone in the GP waiting room, what is this with toilet paper? Ha ha ha. I mean this Covid virus is not stomach flu but chest flu." So many people who don't understand what it is with the toilet paper shortage!

Then I thought, *If everything is symbolic, what would this mean? Maybe it was a dream; it was all pretty surreal. What would it be telling me? I have used this way to frame things, along with awareness of something new being born at this time some call the New Earth Awakening.* It occurred to me in energy work, and it is all the lower chakras! Root chakra bowel shit releasing. The cure? Feeling safe and grounded. Balancing the Solar Plexus stomach, the nourishment center of the body that needs to be anchored. Grounding that energy in daily life, finding that 'still point.' Trusting in divine direction. Taking in energy. Being guided and held by divine will.

So, this is a message for my own healing and injured back, with this narrative being acted out by the collective. In fact, the lockdown that followed gave us all that time to be still. Even the doctor's surgery—the lovely young GP said, "It's stressful at the moment, hard not to take in the collective energies." Indeed, I had an aha moment! While I sat, waiting at the GP, I realized how blessed I am with such health most of the time. Listening, I heard the receptionists replying to phone calls, saying, "You can't come into the GP surgery with flu symptoms. Don't panic. Ring 111 for advice assistance."

I left London in the morning with a dear friend from my school days; we made our way along the coast near where my parents live ... walking with that presence of the divine in each step. There are moments of silence and appreciation of all nature around. I felt happy, and so many people felt my energy, felt our energy. We chatted with people on the coast, a fisherman, and dog walkers and went to a book launch we accidentally stumbled on. I could feel them drawn to the resonance of my friend and me. We had a conversation. It was all light and hope ... tuning into a new wave of flow. So, people smile, and I smile back. So many beautiful conformations are rippling.

> *Today, soul whispered -*
> *Soul, everything is a gift.*
> *You are a gift. We are.*

*Everything is here to help us.*
*So much love unfolding for us.*

**Saturday, March 14**

Meditation at 4 a.m.

Healing self, planet Earth, healing group.

I took myself down to the beach near where my parents live after a morning of nurturing inner being with meditation and healing for self and with group and also for our earth. Feeling so light and well. Appreciate each moment. The pink sky is just there for a few moments, reminding me of how love reflects above and below. True love of all the energies around me. Deeply grounding to Mother Earth, and I appreciate that support too.

I was talking to friends while walking on the beach in Clacton-on-Sea, those in walking group, about a visualization—for fun.

After that, I found a beautiful sheltered spot and, in silence, did both meditation and healing activation. I heard that inner whisper.

> *Do you know how to create connections above and below?*
> *Then activation with God's grace.*
>
> **Release all fear in body**
> **Fear in mind, beliefs past lives and ancestors**
> **Then download into your soul these energetic empowering**
> **beliefs:**
>
> *I am impervious to disease.*
> *I am impervious to illness.*
> *I am impervious to viruses.*
> *I am impervious to collective group consciousness fear.*
> *I am impervious to propaganda.*
> *My immune system is strong.*

*I trust in my body's power to heal and repair itself.*
*I am allowed to defend and protect myself.*
*I am protected; I am safe; I am powerful.*
*I honor and nurture my body.*
*I am worthy mentally, emotionally, physically, and spiritually in all life areas.*

**Stay in the light; claim your holistic wellness. Don't give away your power. Do it for you and all together with friends and family. We are all one. One love, as Bob Marley said, with one heart. I go home and play that song. It makes me smile. So much love to all.**

## Sunday, 15th March

4:44 a.m., meditation. Then qigong, the usual routine basic stance, and grounding, and a bit of 'swimming dragon' movement.

11 a.m.–1.30 p.m.: Starting in Jaywick this time, we got a lift with a sweet soul. We ended up walking the other way to what I usually do when visiting here. Went toward Frinton-on-Sea. The sea showed many faces— rough and dark, light and sparkling. There was para-sailing that was cool to watch ... those who are enjoying these conditions. Accepting and having fun. Our beliefs are powerful indeed: to create much complexity within this drama or to accept, adapt, and move with. This scene illustrates this for me: Walking in a new direction, I see different things. There are three cats that come say hi. There is conversation with others on that walk of beauty of nature, healing, of appreciation.

My attention returns to meditation. I am at peace and a powerful soul, and my mood lifts. Remembering how we feel creates energy of life. This does, of course, manifest. Yet, immunity is simply a thought away.

My soul does not dismiss the power of the subconscious programs that got me all tangled up ... over all that is. To create a unique drama took great focus; to untangle patience, the habit of putting a full stop to the monkey mind. Handing things over to divine source energy that cannot be thought through, I found that they were matched with a powerful magical solution, as I've shifted some of my own behavior and beliefs over the last few weeks ... on immunity particularly.

In the last 24 hours, much more, I say less. Silence is a powerful healer. My parents chose to stop watching so much news. Yay! Before, they were hooked. I notice as I shift in awareness what I see shifting too. They get it; what you feed the energy of you grows.

Today's soul message:

*The response to this current condition/perception of reality is the magic key.*

*A focus on the condition of what we want to create in this world. When you're in it, it's not the energy where we can change it; the shift is to focus on leaving negative patterns.*

*The first step is awareness—getting help. This bit is very hard, and we can have so many blind spots.*

*Step two in my experience is pause. Until you can recalibrate, you just can't make that change required when you're still swimming in the sea of your old life.*

*Step three, surrender to what is. Appreciation of what is from the perspective of this is not what I want. Then I need to take time to heal and be real. What's in the way is the way. In fact, there are a hundred steps I choose from there. Find a safe, quiet place to heal; find your healing support team. Friends to go to tea with, nice hobbies your inner child would approve of. It's about both physical and emotional healing.*

*So, now, I jump in time to November 2022; my life is totally new. So many endings in the midst of new friends, new life, sold flat in London; divorce finished. New projects in community and arts and healing. Raja yoga meditation and qigong healing each day; I also participated in different healing groups around the world with a few dear friends, one of which is Nadene Joy in Canada. I won her competition for guessing the pages of her book ...*

*I dreamt the answer was 88. During that healing, I found a new friend and kindred spirit. We always have similar energy prompts and end up talking once a month. It helps when going through the sticky parts of change to have someone totally outside my direct life to be objective … along with other beautiful souls from people on the way to the 'New me' or maybe I should say the authentic self … Soul sovereign being the mastery of drama queen and wise one, embodying peace and joy in this life. There have been family and friends that have been so supportive here in England too, but my soul asked me to heal and keep this small circle. At times, I had to retreat totally.*

*Indeed, the groups and creative work now are more in alignment with who I am. So, each day continues the process: healing with qigong and walking with the awareness that has led to a new way to paint and draw, eat, drink, speak, move, and see. Now a soul-conscious life, and it's ongoing. There are waves of new impulses … ways to do almost everything with a fresh perspective.*

*I've been taking photos each day too since the lockdown in one place in March 2020. I've really taken this time to become quiet, look, and listen. Nature changes each day, moment-to-moment, and life too. If I can let it change, it can be as easy as deep sleep and a different set of thoughts. Hope, along with faith, appreciation, and gratitude, is key to health and peace and being in each now moment.*

*I've now found a way to enjoy writing because, in the past, due to dyslexia, I stayed away from using it more personally for my creative work, although I used to use it as a designer and lecturer.*

*I write as I speak … It took a lot of inner and external prompts to get me to write; although when working in sketchbooks, word and image often come together. During the lockdown, I read and told 'Stories by the Fire' to adults I loved; these stories were drawn from my lucid dreams and meditation. I shared the images as videos at the Earth Elders Community online 'Story by the Fire' as well as 'Children in Need.' 'Found Object Fairy' joined a fantastic project with Syd Moore, retelling the stories of the women—also a trail—in Manningtree. This is such a huge flip. Creating small local projects that started with a bus but ended up being in a beach hut using the idea of exchange—first, as poetry and art take away. That became an artist residency for Campaign for Equality. I enjoy holding space for other people to tell their stories and create art together in a beach hut in Clacton-on-Sea; that was for families, children, and our inner children from 3–103 years old. I'm very honored to be sharing this story of 'Miracles of Hope.' My focus is both serving the Divine, offering the best of me to continue to heal and nourish the soul and also to share and co-create projects with others.*

*I know my life path has to do with being a creative catalyst; each project based on what I'm learning. At this time, I'm uniting the inner ancient and the inner child and am working on some energy cards for myself. These came day by day when I was going through so much stress. Also, here in Tendring in the UK, that works with trauma. In this way, I pass on what I'm learning. It's been quite tough at times. Honestly, it still is when challenging situations arise. It's through getting the inner script within to shift; creativity; and a return to play, story, and fun that I found my mojo again. Bless your heart; wishing you a cosmic hug from my soul to yours.*

**With infinite love,**

**Kathleen**

## About Kathleen Dutton

Creativity is part of who Kathleen is. We all are 'creative souls.' Her art, events, and courses are all about having fun and going deep within too, opening the door to living your best life with joy.

Kathleen's current focus is co-creating in different settings—multidisciplinary aspects of creativity, healing, and the arts—bringing together community, corporate, and social enterprises both at local and international levels. She has been on BBC Radio talking about her IMAGINE project in Oxford, Sky TV, as well as other social media, and is a regular speaker at international conferences. Her workshops focus on creativity and well-being through storytelling and imagination ... visualization, and creating art in groups through drawing and collage with a focus on show and tell within a circle. A highlight project for her was one at Skylark galleries on the Southbank, London, where she practiced for 19 years. She has worked on creative project partnerships, including cross cultural-branding designs (most recently for Vodafone); graphic designs; illustration storyboards; animations; social media; artist-in-residence; pop-up art events with UAL, Oxo Tower, RSL Collective, Brent Arts, and Libraries.

A particular project of interest was a 'play bus' centered around helping to alleviate isolation, mostly mother and baby and special needs groups. Another project involved 'spirited bodies' and the Society of Designers, Fellowship Kings Fund & Fellowship. The latter two are social enterprise based and were awarded for pioneering leadership at the grassroots level. Others include the Royal Festival Hall and other art and community centers. She spearheaded a project for the homeless and the elderly and worked closely with the Big Issue in and around London and Brent council.

Kathleen's CV includes a position as a lecturer at the University of Westminster, living and working in Hong Kong as a graphic design lecturer at the HK Poly University for seven years and at Conran Design Group for nine years. She has a BA in graphic design from Middlesex University and an MA in visual communications from the University of Central England. She has received three fellowship social enterprise awards for distinction of outstanding work (Fellowship of Chartered Design).

CHAPTER 16

# I Hope You Thrive

Tracey S. Yang

*I hope you heal from the pain in your heart.*
*I hope you flourish.*
*I hope you thrive.*

**My Story of Hope**

My feet hung down as the soles of my shoes pressed against the hardened floor. I had suffered from a chronic illness for over a year now. I looked around to take in my new surroundings since I had never been here before. I wearily sat amongst a group of individuals who had volunteered to pray over me. These people were new to me, so I tried to get to know them. A man from the group sat across from me at the table and opened his mouth to speak. "You are going to find God again," he stated. His statement confused me. *How can I find something that I have never lost?*

...

My new acquaintances brought me to an adjacent room. I stood, and the people circled around me. The group chanted, and one woman spoke in a different language. I did not understand it. How the group prayed for me seemed different compared to how others had prayed for me in the past. I felt their hands firmly pressed against my back. This felt wrong. I could not feel God's love in this place, and a certain heaviness hung in the air. Darkness. The heaviness felt so thick I could almost taste it in my mouth, and I shuddered.

The man in front, the pastor of this small church, raised his hands high and began to do something unimaginable. He called demons forth. He asked them to come. My eyes widened. *What is he doing? Why is he calling them forth?* I wanted to be away from them. I yearned to be soaked in God's presence. The man, the pastor, faced me, while the other members kept their hands on me while continuing to pray. The one woman speaking in a language I didn't understand continued to do so.

The man, the pastor, then spoke aloud, "What is your name?" I looked at him with great confusion, and I kept silent. I didn't quite know what to say. You see, he thought I was possessed, and he made an attempt to communicate to the demon he thought had lived within me. He must not have believed me when I claimed to be Christian.

The group noticed my confusion. Then one of them spoke aloud, "We must pray for the confusion to leave her!"

I panted heavily, my body ready to collapse from sickness and fatigue. The mask I wore due to my weakened immune system fit firmly against my face as I heaved heavily from exhaustion. I had not stood up this long in over a year. Due to the illness I had, I became confined to my bed—my body weight made a quick decline with a loss of nearly 30 pounds. Every time I ventured outside, I became sicker. My immune system was fragile. What they were doing to me crushed my spirit. Tears clung to my eyes, but mere desperation formed within me.

I desperately wanted to be well. I wanted to be healed. The man to the right of me, with his left hand placed on my shoulder, stated, "Have you been rebellious against God?"

I choked on my words, "I'm not perfect, but I try really hard to be a good person." Surely, he was not implying that I had sinned to cause my illness, but he was. This was evident and clear based on the group's earlier actions. They asked me a series of probing questions to see if they could determine how I had sinned. Though I had answered most questions with a no, the group finally told me I was not reading my *Bible* enough. In their minds, this must be how I sinned.

I continued to pant heavily while tears rolled down my face. It pained me, but I let them continue. Due to my desperation and desire to be well, I believed this was going to work. I would rather them deem me as a terrible person than continue suffering from this illness. I wanted God to heal me.

The man to the right of me spoke once again, "The reason why you have not healed yet is that you don't have enough faith." He then stated, "You are struggling to breathe because you have doubts." I cried harder hearing his words.

...

Years passed, and I am now well. I am at the Great Lakes Christian Film Festival with my husband. We were awaiting announcements to see if we had won. The pilot episode we had filmed, "Undying Faith," had been nominated for several awards. The Great Lakes Christian Film Festival is the largest faith-based film festival in the whole state of New York. My heart quickened with anticipation. Yet, still, our names had not been called. Then, finally, it happened. The announcer on stage grinned wide, her silvery dress sparkling as she moved across the carpet. With a microphone in her hand, she yelled, "First place goes to Undying Faith. Congratulations!" I jerked up, my heart still fluttering in my chest. We had won. I smiled brightly and walked on stage to accept our award. I am alive. I am well.

My story is a case of spiritual abuse.

**What is Spiritual Abuse?**

I'm sorry to those that have experienced something similar to me. You did not deserve this. You deserved compassion.

Spiritual abuse is a type of abuse that brings harm. It exists through a pattern of controlling and coercive tactics achieved through the misuse of religion. As well, the perpetrator may misuse religion for selfish or ego-driven endeavors through harassment, humiliation while attempting to dominate others, or other forms of psychological harm. Though not always, at other times, spiritual abuse may come out of a place of ignorance.

It is not uncommon for abusers to misuse scripture to fit the perpetrator's agenda. It is also common for a coercive nature to exist in those who choose to abuse others through a spiritual context.

For children who have experienced spiritual abuse, it is sometimes found in scapegoating. When the child is faced with scapegoating, this child can be singled out and claimed to be rebellious or to be the family's misfortune. A belief that a child is possessed when ill or facing a mental health challenge is also spiritual abuse.

For domestic violence, spiritual abuse is found when an abused wife is advised to become more submissive in order to stop her husband's abuse. If she does decide that she wants to leave, others may try to dissuade her from leaving the marriage by claiming she will be dishonoring God. However, in this case, it is the husband who decided to break his vows when he became abusive. Giving the wife our support, in this case, is what is needed.

Some other common scenarios of spiritual abuse can be found below:

1. Abusers have the desire to position themselves in power. They may claim that God told them to speak to you on His behalf in order to help support their ideas and accusations. There is no room for interpretation of what they are stating to be true or not. The ability to question doctrine is also out of the question. Members may feel pressured to agree to all views a pastor holds. Members who appropriately question incorrect doctrine may be shamed and

bullied. Said members may also be forced into isolation when the pastor asks other members to cut ties with the member that questions incorrect doctrine.

2. A spiritual abuser may claim an individual does not have enough faith or has too many doubts when said individual faces trials in life. This statement may also be used when a growing Christian starts to ask more questions in an attempt to learn more about their faith. This is a sensible endeavor but can cause a spiritual abuser in a pastoral position to feel threatened.

3. When an individual chooses to leave their church, a pastor who spiritually abuses may attempt to isolate and discredit the said person. The person may be gossiped about and be ostracized by others. The spiritually abusive pastor may do this in an attempt to delay other people in the church from leaving.

4. A spiritual abuser may also misuse *Bible* passages in order to justify their abusive actions.

It's not okay.

No one deserves to be abused at church. Church leaders are called to care for the vulnerable and not abuse them. According to biblical passages, church leaders are to lead others based on a high standard.

*"Pay careful attention to yourselves and to all the flock, in which the Holy Spirit has made you overseers, to care for the church of God, which he obtained with his own blood."*

—*Acts 20:28*

*"Not many of you should become teachers, my brothers, for you know that we who teach will be judged with greater strictness."*

—*James 3:1*

*"Keep a close watch on yourself and on the teaching. Persist in this, for by so doing you will save both yourself and your hearers."*

—*1 Timothy 4:16*

### Healing

Spiritual abuse is painful, but there is hope and healing. Below are steps an individual can take to help in the healing process:

1. **Step Away From Where Spiritual Abuse Took Place**

   Many abusers will not take part in helping the injured person heal since self-reflection is often limited within an abuser. No acknowledgment for the harm done will make healing for a survivor more difficult, as acknowledgment for all the harm done is helpful. This is why taking a step away from where spiritual abuse occurred can be a tremendous help. This gives the survivor a chance to heal while they are in a vulnerable state.

2. **Find a Guide**

   Find a trusted guide to help process the trauma. This could be a trusted counselor, a supportive family member, or through self-learning tools. One example of a self-learning tool is this book *Mission Hope*. Other self-learning tools could include—but are not limited to—listening to podcasts, other books about spiritual abuse, or learning information from courses.

3. **Grieve and Process Your Trauma**

   Spiritual abuse is trauma. Take this time to grieve everything. Process what you have lost. The needed time to grieve is different for each survivor. Each survivor will know when the time to let go is right.

4. **Delete the Negative Self-Talk Within**

Abuse can cause a misperception and loss of an accurate self-view. It is not uncommon for a survivor to begin to view themselves in the ways an abuser claimed them to be. This can cause negative self-talk. However, it's important to note that lies are not truth. Take the time to delete the negative, untrue messages within your own mind. Replace the negative messages with truer, positive messages. Every time an untrue message forms within your mind, challenge it. Ask whether this thought is a truth or a lie. For those who are having difficulty distinguishing lie from truth, in this case, talking to your trusted guide can help promote clarity.

5. **Read Scripture**

Read and learn scripture. Do not solely rely on what an authority figure states as truth but also study it for yourself. Ask the Holy Spirit to reveal the true meaning of scripture. Safe individuals will not feel threatened when you try to learn. They will not feel threatened when you desire to learn from multiple sources.

"As he went along, he saw a man blind from birth. His disciples asked him, 'Rabbi, who sinned, this man or his parents, that he was born blind?' 'Neither this man nor his parents sinned,' said Jesus, 'but this happened so that the works of God might be displayed in him. As long as it is day, we must do the works of him who sent me. Night is coming, when no one can work. While I am in the world, I am the light of the world.' After saying this, he spit on the ground, made some mud with the saliva, and put it on the man's eyes. 'Go,' he told him, 'wash in the Pool of Siloam' (this means 'Sent'). So the man went and washed, and came home seeing."

—John 9:1–7

## Supported Biblical Text

John 11:1–32

Job 1–42

Galatians 4:13

John 9: 1–7

Thessalonians 5:11

Romans 8:28

## Definitions and Terms

### Speaking in Tongues

The woman I referred to in my story as speaking in a different language was speaking in tongues. Speaking in tongues is regarded as one of the gifts of the Holy Spirit. To others, the one speaking in tongues may sound as if he or she is speaking in a different language.

## About Tracey S. Yang

 Tracey S. Yang is a thought leader, filmmaker, and published author. Tracey wrote her first book as a co-author for the publication company Motivation Champs, and the book was released in February 2019. The book went on to be a success, with her and her co-authors appearing in podcasts, television, magazines, and other forms of press. The title of this book is *Power Up, Super Women: Stories of Courage and Empowerment.*

After *Power Up, Super Women: Stories of Courage and Empowerment,* Tracey went on to write two other books titled *Gifted Beyond Worlds* and *Mission Hope. Gifted Beyond Worlds* went on to be a best seller while this book, *Mission Hope,* is her third book to be published and released.

Tracey S. Yang currently resides in Alabama, USA, alongside her husband, John, and their two ducks, Woody and Mandy.

Facebook: facebook.com/traceysyang
Twitter: twitter.com/traceysyang
Instagram: instagram.com/traceysyang

**Other Projects by Tracey S. Yang**

### *Undying Faith*

Undying Faith is a Christian television show that focuses on two girls, Lydia Johnson and Joanna Williams, as they must live life in a world without freedom of religion. John Yang, a Hmong filmmaker, created the Christian television show, and the production company behind Undying Faith is Kyo Production.

**Website**: undyingfaith.kyproduction.com

### *Daily Talk Catalog*

Daily Talk Catalog is a digital magazine and shop that emphasizes positive and uplifting content. It promotes healing, connectivity, and encouragement.

**Website:** dailytalkcatalog.com

### *Kyo Production*

Kyo Production is a media production company based in Alabama and founded by John Yang. Kyo Production is most known for their production of the Christian television show, Undying Faith, which has won many awards from top based Christian film festivals such as Best Series at the Great Lakes Christian Film Festival and Best Television and Web-First Time Filmmaker at Content Film Festival and News Media Summit.

**Website:** kyoproduction.com

# CHAPTER 17

# What Matters Most is
# What Matters Most - JOY!

Minnku Buttar

Most fairy tales end with "and they lived happily ever after!" This fixation on happiness being epitomized in the standard fairy tale as an end product confuses our psyche as does the notion that 'joy and happiness' sits coiled in a corner, to be picked up once you reach certain pre-determined notions of success benchmarks defined by you for yourself or by what the society subscribes for your existence. Let me tell you that the beauty of it all is that there is actually no happy ending as such. ("When the dung dries, the worms are finished, however much progress they may have made." —Nisargadatta Maharaj)

So, the imagined happy ending, the promise of a permanent, personal state of perpetual happiness and bliss, called 'Enlightenment' (Moksha) by some, doesn't really fit with the way reality is. Think of an ocean. The waves in the ocean are no wetter or closer to the ocean than any other, and no wave has an independent existence; all of them are the same ever-changing, undivided, seamless movement of the ocean. Similarly, there is no permanent person to be permanently enlightened. Sit with this statement for a moment, and it becomes self-evident.

In fact, what is proposed by French philosopher, Pierre Teilhard de Chardin, is also the emphatic conclusion of my long and arduous journey that we are not human beings striving to be spiritual; we are already spiritual beings, eternal souls, born into this physical world to have a human experience; we are light and will merge into light. And I think of my last breath often, with amusement and wonderment. When the time comes, will I embrace my subtle body's merging with the divine source with excitement, or will I resist, stamp my feet as an errant child and say (to whoever it is who will come and fetch me), "Nah, not leaving because my work here on the planet is not done yet"?

Just to make things confusing, here's another twist to the human pursuit of happiness. The inference of Dr. Martin Vestergaard (a cognitive and behavioral neuroscientist at Cambridge University), who has been studying brain mechanisms underlying suboptimal behavior and irrational decision-making, makes is that humans prefer experiences with happy endings (a phenomenon known as the 'happy ending effect') to experiences that became slightly less enjoyable toward the end. The culprit amygdala (two almond-shaped clusters in the right and left hemispheres of the brain) preserves and processes different pieces of information from the same experience, which implies that an ongoing happy experience can be marred if it doesn't end well.

Interesting. Since happiness seems more short-lived and momentary, driven by our 'happy ending' effect, my perpetual quest has become seeking, persevering for something that is more sustained, uplifting feeling and experience.

And when I say persevere, I mean really look hard as if trying to find a long-lost diamond studded needle in a haystack. Imagine you finally find it and realize that it's brilliant, more precious, and magical than you thought, that it has the power to change the lens through which you view the world; it brings utter harmony to your thoughts, speech, and actions; it helps restore your faith in humanity, takes inventory of your heart-centered values with empathy, shatters the illusionary ego, unlearns sense of judgments, and allows you to live with dignity. Then you hear it whispering gently in your ears, "Hey, gentle soul … my name is Joy. I live in every single mindful moment of your normal, mundane day, so trust me; breathe, pause, treat your miseries with respect, and quit today to come back stronger tomorrow!" Wow!

And if you are anything like me, sensation-thrill-seeking, with a tendency to pursue new and different novel sensations, feelings, and intense experiences (border-line adrenaline junkie, as I call myself), the 'idea' of this magic that Joy promises is probably appealing as you read this. But don't be fooled so fast because the road to becoming a whole person in mind-body-spirit and bringing out the healthiest, joyful version of yourself needs you to become a witness to a reborn balance and 'reclaim the self.' It will need bravery and courage because the world can be unkind, and fear, jealousy, and anger fuel the actions of those who wish to assert their power and eliminate those they deem unworthy.

So, for now, I suggest, breathe, pause. Till one day, two choices become inevitable. First, you can embrace this reclamation—by force or by empathy—allowing the tides to shift. Or, secondly, you allow yourself to drown in toxicity, self-pity, and the eternal diminishing of self-worth, the resurrection of which can take a lifetime. I suggest going with the first choice—conscious reclamation of self and your place in this world, where no longer will those around us decide if we deserve to exist.

I have walked this path consciously—rising above the psyche of living as a bare survivor to start living a life that matters and aligns with my purpose to be a mature and compassionate contributor to the world (as guided by my dearest mentor Swami Dayananda Saraswati ji) because, at the end of life, what really matters is not what we bought but what we built; not what we got, but what we shared; not our competence, but our character; and not our success, but our significance. So, be prepared to walk this windy road of healing and doing some 'uncomfortable deep work' on yourself, for to get something you never had means taking action to do something you've never done before. Sounds like an intense journey. It is, as I found out.

## My Hope Story

> "In order to realize the miracle of what you are, you must
> surrender the fantasy of what you will become."
>
> —*Ram Tzu*

All of us have unique stories and wonderful opportunities to see beyond ourselves, even in the bleakest moments, braided in hope and resilience. I want to share mine from those times when those around me saw me with a smile that only stayed for a little while, only to drown in a deep ocean of despair and sorrow. I was grasping for air and hoping it would get better tomorrow, while I knew that my self-esteem diminished by the day, tears and rage becoming a norm, with that horrible empty feeling at the pit of the stomach that makes you think you mean nothing to this world. If you can relate to those sentiments—feel distressed, anxious, challenged, fearful, not good enough, and uncertain of the future—I think you may relate to this story.

Telling our story is a process rooted in truth, reconciliation, and courage, lending hope and encouragement to others to open up conversations. A collective acknowledgment to heal and repair on an individual level so that we may use this healing to serve as a key stepping-stone in our evolution toward collective healing for humans and the planet as a whole.

I am blessed to be born into a Sikh religion that stresses on selfless service or volunteerism, professes universal love, encourages altruism, and promotes compassion. We all grow up being witnesses to the fact that service to others (Seva - serving the house of God and humanity) is an essential core and aspect of devotional practice for the laity and not the virtuosos. It is the everyday worshipper, and not the ordained priests, who are the heroes. Not the great, the gifted, the sage who serves ordinary people, but it is ordinary people who serve ordinary people. Starting from the person who puts away your shoes at the temple gates through the person who assiduously sweeps the temple floors to those who stand over hot fires in the kitchen to feed bountiful 'langar' (free meals); they are all heroes. Sikh gurdwaras (Temples—places of worship) are spotlessly clean, and there is a shelter for all because devotees practice compassionate service as a routine religious act, and not as a deliberated heroic act. But, first, where it all started.

My teens were almost eventless, happy, and carefree. A flying distinction in Economics Honors from university, a selective friends' social circle; all seemed fine. At the age of 22, I succumbed to my parents' wishes to marry a match they chose. The next 17 years saw me in a flamboyant expatriate lifestyle, dozens of holidays each year, spiffy residences in eight global wonderful locations, and a life with vibrant ex-pat communities. Because we all were in the same boat, we derived sustenance and strength from our relationships, and irrespective of our diplomatic corps, UN or oilfield backgrounds, we all connected over shared experiences and interests, with promises of lifelong connections.

Countries like Nigeria, Myanmar, and Indonesia had very little to offer in terms of urban infrastructure and clubs, and boredom becomes the reverse side of fascination, so most of our blithesome evenings were spent exchanging amusing tales from our respective countries. Having grown up in seven cities (as an 'Air Force brat'—offspring of an armed forces officer), I pulled up fascinating, never-ending tales and contextual stories that I had grown up with—about the assertive and multifarious Hindu belief of the inviolability of animals and the status of gods and goddesses given to them in ancient Indian literary texts. I would get asked often, "Is it true that cows still walk freely on Indian roads?" (*Duh! Yes*, I thought silently).

My favorite tales were about deities' association with cows—Krishna (the cowherd god), Shiva (the bull rider), and Kamadhenu (goddess considered the 'mother of all cows'). Another of my popular story was about Karni Mata Temple ('Temple of Rats,' in which over 25,000 rats meander about and inhabit crevices, often passing over the feet of the visitors and devotees; consuming items that have been nibbled on by these rats is regarded as a holy practice here); and how Lord Vishnu incarnated in the form of a fish (Mathsya), amphibious Turtle (Kurma), and a boar (Varaha).

Each country I lived in has contributed to my growth. In Venezuela, we, expatriate wives, were taught tactical taekwondo moves and the art of situational awareness to combat frequent kidnappings and carjacking. (The ex-FBI agents who taught these classes told us clearly that there is usually little or no time for deliberation, so learning self-defense was not an option.) I thought carjackings were mostly a trope from 1970s' action movies till I was held at gunpoint one day while picking up kids from their school, but that's a story for another time.

One day, in Nigeria, I witnessed a terrifying mob lynching incident, 'jungle justice,' as they call it. Apparently, the thief they caught was to be burnt to death, and as I arrived on the scene on the school bus, they had just set fire to the rubber tire he was tied to. Shocking and brutal— and a disregard for the fact that victims may be innocent and merely in the wrong place at the wrong time. It left me terrified to step out of the arm-guarded communities we all ex-pats lived in.

In the Philippines, we were the victims of a foul robbery, and in Indonesia, I foiled an attempt to kidnap my son in a supermarket.

Each experience enriched and taught me resilience, courage, humility, resourcefulness, and street-smartness, and I learned how composure; awareness; and paying attention to people, situations, and your environment will get you out of the toughest and trickiest situations. I am living affirmation and validation that there is no better way to imbibe the art of inclusivity, patience, respect, and appreciation of human connections than by the total cultural immersion that can only happen by living with diverse cultures.

Unfortunately, deep inside, I was feeling empty and lonely; I was in despair over the lack of companionship, understanding, and support. It felt like life's cruelest irony. I vividly remember being hit by waves of disbelief and confusion, amongst constant gasping for air through uncontrollable sobs, thinking all the time, *How, after all, can you be married and lonely?*

"The most terrible poverty is loneliness
and the feeling of being unloved."

—*Mother Teresa*

Constant loneliness accompanies your every waking and sleeping hour; it arrests the blood flowing to and from your heart when you share your deepest feelings with your spouse and long for attention and love, only to have them disregarded, disparaged, or derided. I loved life and was gregarious. Laughter matters to me. Humor functions like an automatic safety valve in my pressure cooker that has always prevented the building up of excessive pressures and intense anxieties in my life. Being silly matters to me. Being with good people matters to me. But when I look back and reflect, I still don't understand how I ended up in a vicious circle of nastiness, zillion misunderstandings, and harsh conflicts with my then-husband.

I think your heart scars forever, throwing you in a spate of self-doubts and self-pity, and I wish fervently that I knew then what I do now—that by communicating and expressing more emphatically, we take our power back and help meet our partner's needs too. It's a two-way street. None of us were bad people. Immature, yes, and it kept us from being what we wanted to be as a couple.

"A little foolishness, enough to enjoy life, and a little wisdom to
avoid the errors, that will do."

—*Osho*

This emotionally tumultuous phase in my marriage also coincided with the all-consuming role I had also inadvertently taken up as a codependent and traumatized caretaker of my own dysfunctional family of origin. My inherent compassionate nature and zeal to be the ultimate emotional support for my family sucked me into a black hole of an inordinate amount of worrying and desperation to fix the distressed, manipulative, abusive, and highly toxic environment created between my parents, two siblings, and a vindictive and manipulative (borderline wicked) sister-in-law. I had no knowledge or a divine angel in my life that could guide me through this upside-down roller-coaster ride to learn detachment of some sort in order to regain some emotional headroom space.

It didn't help that both my mother and sister were under acute depression at that time, and the fear of receiving terrible news every time the phone rang at odd nighttime hours would bring nausea and bile up in my mouth. And even though I lived thousands of miles away from India, I would jump onto a flight many times to be there in person to resolve their ugly conflicts and ugly crisis, leaving me lonelier than ever and with no one to discuss my own marital struggles. Could I have saved my marriage if my parents had become my mediators? Perhaps. Who knows?

After a nasty incident of physical violence between my dad and my already fragile mom, I was forced to take a stance against a disparaging typical patriarchal and egoistic father and his inherent dominating ideologies. That was the start of a landslide relationship with him. Nothing I did after that would ever make him see my value and strengths.

Life dealt me with shocking blows when I lost both my mother and sister in the space of 10 years. They chose to be architects of their lives and wrote their own scripts. The anguish, I know, truly stays with you till you die. I have bled to death 100 times since then, and no one can even imagine how deep the unseen scars can be. A year later, one afternoon, while lying on the bed, with my eyes closed, I felt her tender fingers scrape my hand as if letting me know that I had grieved enough and it was time to move on bravely. 17 years later, I can still smell her fragrance in the silk saree that I preciously treasure and her fleeting touch on my fingers when I hug it.

With dad's passing a few years ago, the heritage I inherited is a lifelong responsibility of a bipolar brother, whose bouts of hypomania, psychotic mania, and clinical depression over the years have been exhausting as a caretaker. I wasn't finished with this world yet. I told it: "Bring it on!!!"

I was now back in India. Divorced. We parted amicably. My older son was in a boarding school in Australia, and my 14-year-old daughter was with me for a time. I had yet another sacrifice to make when I allowed her to shift to Australia at her dad's request. I was again alone and lonely.

I chose to settle in the charming city of Bangalore, located in Southern India on the Deccan Plateau, with its flaming-red Transport Service buses and the Gulmohar (mayflower) trees in full bloom in the temperate April showers.

Strangely, I was struggling to adjust to my own country, and the territory felt 'unknown' and uncomfortable. I was baffled too. When I look back, I attribute my resistance to factors that irked me: the incessant horns in the unruly traffic, the potholes on the road, and the exaggerated male egos with the exaggerated judgment of their capabilities and importance. They were off-putting.

I was also taken aback and jolted by a subtle underlying separatist attitude from some older Bangloreans I had met. I heard jibes and diatribes like: "You North Indians come to Bangalore and spoil our culture, complain and complain as if your Delhi roads are laid in gold!" I'm not implying the entire city has a mean streak. So, please, don't get me wrong. Bangalore is a tale of two cities, of two kinds of people: the intelligent, hospitable, and kind who set an example in selflessness and charity, and then there's the immigrant-hating jingoistic kind with a huge attitude.

> "The intuitive mind is a sacred gift and the rational mind
> is a faithful servant. And I thought …
> What if our society has forgotten this gift?"
>
> —*Einstein*

## The Blossoming

I knew that some deep transformational work was needed immediately to heal from the bleeding wounds of losing a mom, a younger sister, and a dad; the aftermath of a divorce; and a very wounded inner child. We run and hide, but when tragedy and challenges enter our lives and start speaking to the parts of ourselves that are struggling, striving with self-doubt, dark closets with skeletons open up, and it requires bad-ass courage to deal with them. I was feeling a new faith and strength in my soul, a gentleness derived from self-love I call 'grace.'

"Faith is a knowledge within the heart, beyond the reach of proof."

—*Kahlil Gibran*

And in this knowing and believing, I became this thirsty, in-exhaustive seeker perpetually searching, longing, pining, prostrating, and praying—with the intention to invite the right people into my life. My next few years became a journey of 'deep work'—a reconstruction of my perforated emotional energy that comes from relentless destruction. This dealing with my demons headlong made me a witness to the change of my own trajectory—a heady mix of curiosity, fear, and curiosity!

I feel blessed with the evolved masters the universe granted me. Their love filled my empty and forlorn voids and guided me to retrieve and reclaim my own power, grit, and resilience during those most challenging times.

My 'pranams' (heartfelt salutations) to Master Dhyan Vimal. (In the days of complete chaos and despair following the unexpected loss of my mom, Master and his tribe literally adopted me in love and through his teachings of the "6 Rites of Creation"—disciplines and awareness one needs to actualize the promise of what one can be and to wake up to exist as a creator and effector of your life.)

Pujya Sri Swami Dayananda Saraswati ji. (A globally renowned teacher of Vedanta, who, metamorphically speaking, adopted me and gave me love, guidance, and opportunities to cook for him and dine with him on his table. The retreats at Arsha Vidya Pitham Ashram, on the banks of the Holy Ganga, and in Anaikatti—near Coimbatore, South India, where I dived into Vedanta and Upanishads—lent me the distraction-free concentration and self-discovery time that I needed. I took the opportunity to travel further north in the Himalayas to visit other saints or meditate in dark caves with only bats as company.)

I met this demure teacher Phyllis Krystal twice when she visited India to share 'The Phyllis Krystal Method,' a visualization method that uses techniques, rituals, and symbols that rely on an inner source of security and wisdom and can be used to offset negative conditioning, old behavior patterns, fears, limitations, and inner blocks. Even though there were hundreds of attendees for her facilitation and accreditation sessions, I was blessed to spend one-on-one time and receive special guidance. That was a soothing balm from my emotional exhaustion.

## The Journey Continues

What did my journey bring me? How am I leading my life? The universe is asking, "Show me your new vibration; I will show you miracles."

Firstly, our universe's higher energies are integrating within our consciousness like never before, and as part of humanity's collective consciousness, zeroing into what/who uplifts your energy, what/who zaps it, and cutting out all that is toxic (people, thoughts, habits) becomes our personal responsibility. Only when our frequencies vibrate on higher energy can we become contributors to planet earth. So, I have consciously become a witness to experience the 'eternal dance' and reality of the mind's consciousness, perception, sensation, and my own reactions to all stimuli around me.

Secondly, we must truly heal at the cellular level, and that will mean re-opening old wounds, burning old illusions, and a courageous confrontation with our pain, for in that darkness, you will encounter your wounded inner child. And if you were raised with only conditional love—meaning you had to meet certain conditions and criteria in order to be loved, cherished, or valued—then that is how you're fulfilling and showing up in your adult life too. 'Cutting Ties' with my wounds and lingering traumas (as taught by my mentor Phyllis Krystal) connected me with the here and now; it brought me closures to conflicts, confusions, antagonisms, and attachments to the idea of being 'hurt' as well as attachments to those ideations. After so many years, irrespective of my brokenness, I was falling in love with myself, knowing fully that I will never allow anyone to ever dull my sparkle again.

Thirdly, I have forgiven all who contributed to my 'injured-ness' over the years. Resentment, grudges, unjustified judgments, and anger trap your life energy, limit you, and make moving forward difficult—like trying to ride a bicycle with the brakes partly on all the time. As I often say, "If you don't deal with past hurt and traumas, they will deal with you!" So, why carry baggage? Be selfish and drop them. Reserve your time, intensity, and spirit exclusively for those who reflect sincerity. I want my garb to be strength and dignity. Can you see it, feel it?

> "Darkness cannot drive out darkness; only light can do that. Hate cannot drive out hate; only love can do that."
>
> —*Martin Luther King, Jr.*

Fourthly, developing a 'grateful disposition' has not only been a social glue fortifying my relationships but has also inculcated optimism, joy, humility, and surrendering to "what will be will be." Fearlessly and curiously, I am exploring this new-found oneness and harmony I feel with others. Like all of us, I am living on borrowed time, light wanting to merge with light. So, I want to exist with an intimate, restful, yet curious connection with the world. I am willing to allow life to unfold at its own pace.

Fifthly, the key to the paradox is within us all. It's called 'unconditional love.' Too often we underestimate the power of a touch, a smile, a kind word, a listening ear, an honest compliment, or the smallest act of caring, all of which have the potential to turn a life around. I have been waiting for a new dawn and tribe till I saw "A Gathering of the Tribe" (a powerful short film by Charles Eisenstein w/Jon Hopkins and Aubrey Marcus), and I know that the longing in my heart is an intuitive knowledge that even though loneliness, betrayal, drudgery, anxiety, the pain of separation, and degradation seem normal right now, we will witness the burst of the miraculous flame from the inextinguishable spark that lies in all of us; we will find our tribe again. For now, I allow the veil from my eyes to be torn, wipe the mirror of my mind clean, and allow the doors of perception to stay open.

"You are That already."

—*wise sage Sri Nisargadatta Maharaj*

What if this, right here, right now—this one eternal present moment— is it? What if life will always be a mix of positive and negative, pain and pleasure, success and failure, enlightenment and delusion, nirvana and samsara? What if there is no beginning and no end? And what if there is space here/now for all of it to be just as it is?

What if joy is a sustained experience in this 'now'? What a relief!

## Who am I today?

Today, I thrive as a travel junkie. My mantra: Journey. Explore. Discover. Repeat. Go to places out of comfort zone. Thrilling destinations that spark joy: para-gliding from 8,000 ft in Switzerland; white-water rafting down big drops in the rapids of the Kaituna River in Cairns; snorkeling in coral reefs of the Great Barrier Reef (the richest ecosystems of the world); magical horse-riding in magical sunrises in Gold Coast (through hidden beaches and creek crossings through rainforest, river bush, and cane fields); hot-air balloon rides in Cappadocia (over stunning volcanic valleys and landscape); chasing the Northern Lights in Finland (the Aurora Borealis); being mesmerized by the shooting stars in the night skies of Nubra Valley (Sumur sand dunes, Ladakh); climbed to pristine Gurudwara Sri Hemkunt Sahib Ji (most revered Sikh shrines in Himalayas at an altitude of around 4,329); accomplished the arduous 14-day journey and ultimate pilgrimage to Kailash-Mansarovar (considered Shiva's abode at high altitude of 19,000 feet above sea level); and, in October of 2022, finally manifested a 29-year-old fetish to speak at a TEDx. I include it in this list because it was quite a journey to prepare for it, and, coincidentally, it was the sixth most-watched talk of November 2022.

## There is no 'Ending'

"Perplexity is the beginning of knowledge."

*—Kahlil Gibran*

Life has been a rollercoaster recently, emotionally flooded, and healing chapters have re-opened again after I lost my best friend (aged 59) to Covid in 2021, and my eldest sister lost her fight with cancer in 2020. I am pausing through the fog of my loss and grief, treading on the path to healing respectfully and with dignity. (Truthfully? Nothing lessens the total weight of grief somehow. Time is a great healer, it is said. I wait and watch.)

The balancing aspect is that I have re-married, am good friends with my ex, my kids are doing well at their jobs in Australia, and I feel healthy and blessed.

In this poem I composed a while ago, I encapsulate my way of new-found belief and thought form. I share it in great humility!

### WINGS OF HOPE

*Bodies but frail vessels—our life interconnected to trees, birds, winters, the universe—with time limited on earth, I ponder secretly in solitude about my soul,*

*Of an existence so unique, irreplaceable, embracing consciously chosen attitudes—that illuminate pitch-dark perspectives—welcoming openness as a flavor of life as a whole.*

*Breaking free of chains of melancholy—sometimes in anguish and apprehensions, I drown, but in gratitude of existential blessings of grace, I rise with an unfathomable vision wider than abilities profound,*

*Small ray of self-love rises—an uplifting realization of axes not ground, judgments avoided, ego battles ignored, power agendas undefined—refusing imprisonment of my own mind's sound.*

*Today I bedazzle—radiate, glimmer, scintillate, deflect—rejecting senses of injury for the injury itself to disappear; dispel doom to rise above gloom; inject a bright glow of hope,*

*In a powerless indecisive life, we cannot die; instead, carry enthusiastic spirit of a child into our graves, step into secrets of our geniuses—alleged impossibilities treated as opportunities before they elope.*

*When cold winds of cruel fate speak—support others with a soulful wonder of the luminous morning dew—our tongues dipped in delectable nectar of love on the universe we can shower,*

*A momentous leap beyond biases—shattering the prism of racial differences; thinking of another, not in pity but empathy—acknowledge their need for love no less than ours.*

*If souls unify in common blood, would universal love be still imprisoned behind hidden agendas and malice? Our own validations questioned—raise collective human consciousness without strife.*

*Hope never abandoned—a joyful rainbow, a pedagogy of peace, our yearning for deep connections—our allegiance to spread cheer we can pledge while still on the edge of life!*

*I have miles to go before I sleep, so I ask myself if what I did today is getting me closer to where I want to be tomorrow. In that, I rest.*

## About Minnku Buttar

Professionally, I am humbled that I achieved my 29-year-old wish list to speak at a TEDx. I am a national award-winning transformation and mindfulness facilitator, healer, intuitive life coach, international keynote speaker, advanced pranic and kriya yoga initiate, a Tibetan bowls sound healer, contemporary artist, curator and designer for events, panelist and jury, and emcee on many platforms.

As founder of The Circle of Joy (offering self-mastery programs and retreats) and through a very well-received YouTube talk titled "Stories and Secrets From Around the World," I help motivate others so that they may heal, flourish, and nourish their souls. As a mentor and strategic advisor for many NGOs, I passionately address subjects of art, culture, and women empowerment, impacting thousands of women in India.

I co-authored an anthology *Diversity – it changes the perspective you see the world with*, part of the Global Intellectual Series, recognized by *Scholars Book of World Record*, 2022. I'm a columnist in a New York based lifestyle, art, and culture magazine called "Womensstraighttalk." I also write for the popular platform "BUSINESSWOMEN 360°."

I'm humbled to have won a few national awards: Sashakt Naari Samman (influencer of 2022); Stri Shakti award, 2021 (Telangana government); women of excellence award and iconic woman 2020 (The Women Economic Forum); Swami Vivekananda award: change maker of 2020.

CHAPTER 18

# Finding Hope, Happiness, and Meaning in Life

—

## Jennifer Bassett

I grew up around adults who used substances (one grandmother religion) in life in order to cope and be happy. Both my parents were alcoholics, and so I was raised as a child by my dad's sister. She saved me from having to go into the foster care system. The environment I was raised in impacted me in such a way that I chose to begin drinking alcohol at the age of 11.

I have searched for happiness in substances, relationships, religion, and work, and finally, at age 55, I discovered that happiness is a state of being, not a destination. How did I find this belief? At age 48, I was diagnosed with MS, and life as I knew it changed. I became so depressed that I thought about ending my life. It was the love of my six beautiful children that helped me realize the example I would be leaving them of how to cope when life gets tough. It was time to break the cycle I had grown up in.

There is no magic happy pill, relationship, financial reward, or career that makes you truly happy. Yes, these things can bring us happiness but not the kind that lasts.

There are 10 steps I practice that make me feel happy and fulfilled in my life, and this feeling is just too amazing not to share with all who are looking to find hope, happiness, and meaning in their lives!

1.  Alcohol and drugs don't bring us happiness! In fact, they bring with them a whole world of hurt such as infidelity, financial problems, the breakup of families, violence, etc. Now, I'm not saying that having a glass of wine or a cocktail to celebrate is wrong; I'm talking about using alcohol or drugs to cope with life and/or to numb out and not feel. I learned this from a few seasons in my life where I turned to alcohol for the wrong reasons, and it made my issues worse, not better. The latest time was when I found out my ex-husband had sexually molested my older daughters. He went to prison, and I sold our home in Alaska and bought a new home in Utah so we could move closer to our family. I boarded a plane, destination Utah, as a newly single mom with six children ages 15, 13, 10, 5, 3, and a toddler. I made it through all of this, but life didn't get any easier in Utah working full-time as a nurse and as a single parent. It began with me allowing myself to have a drink or two occasionally when the stress got high, which then evolved into every weekend, then began the one or two glasses of red wine after work. Before I knew it, alcohol had become a way to cope, just like the examples I saw growing up. Life will never be completely stress-free, but we can find healthy ways to cope vs. unhealthy ways.

2.  In order to learn how to truly love another person unconditionally, we have to first learn how to love ourselves. When we were born, we knew how to love ourselves. Have you ever seen a baby kissing his reflection in the mirror? What happens is, the world slowly chips away at your ability to love yourself for your authentic self. You really have to learn how to love and care for yourself because, in this hustle and bustle world, there is no time for you, unless you make

'you' a priority! This was something I didn't fully understand until I became sick with MS. Please don't wait till you get sick to begin this important practice of loving and caring for yourself. It makes you a better human being, mom, employee, friend, spouse, and sibling. So, pencil in an essential oil, salt bath, or bubble bath soon.

3. A healthy lifestyle, as well as your fork, can literally transform your life. It did mine! I suffered from depression and anxiety, a bonus that comes with MS, and since I changed my diet and lifestyle, I feel happy the majority of my days and less anxious. When I was diagnosed with MS, I was 130 lbs. overweight, a diet coke addict, and I ate a lot of the western diet with too many carbohydrates and did far too little exercise. I was a nurse manager for a very busy home-care agency. Stress management consisted of a daily glass or two of red wine after the kids had been taken care of and falling asleep in front of the television, waking up, and doing it all over again. I felt like a robot. It took me getting sick to wake up and realize I wasn't living the life I wanted. I wanted more for my life, and my children deserved the best version of me. So, I began eating a healthier diet, and I slowly started making lifestyle changes. I kept the practices that worked and discarded what didn't. What a difference five years of doing this has made. It was the best thing I've ever done!

4. Spirituality is found within when you are able to recognize and process your emotions in a healthy way. We are multidimensional beings, and it's important that we find a balance between our mind, body, and spirit. Some of my family on both parents' sides were Mormon, and I had a grandmother on my dad's side who felt it was her duty to impose her beliefs on all her children and grandchildren. It negatively impacted my dad, my sister, and me. Religion is great for connecting people who have similar beliefs, but it cannot make you spiritual. This is a personal connection between you and whatever you believe is your higher power. For me, it is God, and I have

found inner peace from developing my spiritual relationship through prayer and meditation. Meditation has really helped me to silence the incessant chatter in my mind, think clearer, and get in touch with my spiritual side.

5. Human connection is vital to our overall well-being. This was a hard one for me because I'm a lot like my dad and can be a loner. My children helped me with this, as it's hard to remain a loner when raising six children, especially when I became a single mother. Are you finding it hard to find friends or feel connected? Go online and find a group to join or volunteer for a cause you feel strongly about. Studies have even shown that people who lack human connection may be at risk for Alzheimer's type dementia.

6. Perfection doesn't exist! If you want to do something, don't wait for the perfect moment, or you will wait your life away. I was a perfectionist for years and drove myself mad! I missed out on opportunities because I never felt ready. I always made it a practice to praise my children for all their accomplishments because, no matter what I did growing up with my aunt, it was never good enough. An A should have been an A+. I was never skinny or pretty enough, but in fairness, she learned this from her mother, my grandmother, who was very critical of me growing up. I now live by an 80/20 rule in my life, and it has helped me immensely by quieting what I like to call my 'inner psycho.'

7. What people think about you is none of your business. What matters is what the person in the mirror thinks about you. Live your authentic truth. Date to be different and choose the roads less traveled. Too many times I have dimmed my light, played small, and as a result, I've missed out on some great opportunities.

8. A romantic relationship requires 100% commitment from both members. Going into a marriage with the idea that you can abort at any

time does not foster a lasting relationship. It helps to explore your attachment style and how you've learned to be loved. I have sabotaged relationships not being aware of my own, and it has cost me a marriage and the love of my life. This is material for a whole book in itself. I do not claim to be an expert on this subject, but I'm sharing what I have learned because a meaningful, loving relationship is something I desire in the future, and I know I'm not alone. I didn't always have the best opinion of men because of a lot of unresolved anger toward the male role models in my life. I was also so bitter after what my ex-husband put me and my children through that I wasted many years and made some foolish decisions.

9. It's okay to love being a mother and grandmother. I was raised where women were hitting the workforce full force, and wanting to stay home to raise your kids was not considered being ambitious. My mother was not around when I was little, and she was never able to be a hands-on grandma. In fact, she was still dating when I had some of my kids, so she didn't like us to call her grandma. I pledged I would be more involved not only in my children's lives but the lives of my grandchildren. I was able to stay home with three of my kids while babies, and the other three, I worked part- to full-time. What a difference it made in the amount of time I had, and it meant prioritizing my time and sometimes missing out on things I wish I hadn't. Being on the run all the time between working and kids' activities made it so our diets weren't always healthy either. It was easy to run by McDonald's for the happy meals when you only had a half hour to eat dinner. The more we were on the run, the more we tended to make less nutritious choices. It's truly a gift nowadays to be able to stay at home, if you choose to, and raise your children. It isn't for everyone, though, and if that is you, don't dare beat yourself up. I did it, and my children still love me. My children, and now grandchildren, are my greatest treasures in life.

10. Gratitude is the attitude to change all others. I make it a practice before I get out of bed to think of five things I'm grateful for. When I'm being really good, I write in a gratitude journal. I also try to find one new thing I'm grateful for every day. I know it sounds simple, but it works! Try it for 30 days.

Developing MS later in life forced me to slow down and take a deep inventory of my life. I'm truly grateful for this experience because I found how to be happier and more fulfilled. My *hope* is that if you are seeking the same, you'll find it here in this book.

In closing, I would like to share with you 10 habits I find that really make a difference in my overall health and happiness:

1. Daily gratitude practice. You can start a gratitude journal or just develop a personal practice that feels meaningful to you.

2. Daily meditation and/or prayer. There are so many different styles of meditation, so find one that works for you. The goal is to silence the mind. Deep breathing exercises are also very helpful. I practice deep breathing throughout the day when I need to quiet my mind, refocus, or deal with something stressful.

3. Move your body every day. Whether inside your home, in a gym, or outside. I love walking five days a week, but in the winter, when it's really cold, I don't always get out, so I ordered a mini trampoline for Christmas.

4. Hydrate every day. The minimum is 64 ounces a day. Use a filter to clean heavy metals and chlorine from your water.

5. Learn to love yourself and put yourself first by practicing an act of self-care daily. Do one small act of self-care daily; it doesn't have to be something big. This will increase your ability to love and care for yourself.

6. Practice the 80/20 rule in life. For example, eat healthy 80 percent of the time and allow yourself to splurge 20 percent of the time. You

don't need to be 100% perfect, and it's not possible, so save yourself a lot of stress. Give yourself permission to be perfect 80 percent of the time and imperfect 20 percent.

7. Practice an act of kindness daily. A random act of kindness is my favorite. The world so needs this, and it makes someone else feel good as well as yourself. Donate your time or resources to charities you resonate with. Also, reach out and make new connections with other humans and strengthen existing relationships.

8. Practice forgiveness for your own peace of mind. Even if you can't bring yourself to forgive right now, just the desire to do so helps bring comfort to your inner being.

9. Focus on what's good in the world. As Tony Robbins says, what's wrong is always available, but so is what's right. I'm not saying that you should not be aware or help make a difference when you can, but our energy flows where our focus goes. Your time and energy are precious resources, so ask yourself where you want to spend your energy, then change your focus to that thing.

10. Personal development is so important to help us become the best version of ourselves and to accomplish our dreams/goals. Mindset plays a key role. Daily affirmations are helpful to me to help me keep my mindset and focus where I want them to be. I also try to carve out time daily for activities that help me grow as a person. Even if you only have 15 minutes a day, it will be so worth it.

## About Jennifer Bassett

I'm a 55-year-old retired RN, USAF veteran, nurse health coach, and a mother of six adult children, with two grandsons who are the absolute joy of my life. I was diagnosed with MS at age 48 and had to quit the nursing profession two years later after multiple exacerbations left me unable to work. I have been on a healing journey for the past five years, and I've transformed from being completely depressed and ready to give up to being happy and fulfilled. Life didn't change; I changed … and that has made all the difference. My passion now is to help others find the path to wellness through lifestyle changes and what they put at the end of their forks.

# CLOSING

In this book, I am thrilled to have had the opportunity and privilege to share with you 18 power-filled stories packed with years of wisdom from the experiences of learned leaders in their unique fields.

These insightful, inspiring stories were written with authenticity and vulnerability,

all to give you hope and the tools necessary to help you find yourself, your inner power, and your special gifts to truly be who you are. For you to know you are good enough, you are brave enough to do and be anything that you want to. Yes, you! We believe in you! Now, it's time for you to believe in yourself.

When I say "Learn to find the gift in everything ... even the not-so-good stuff," I mean it. But what does it mean? It means that through all your trials and tribulations, there is truly a gift. I believe every single thing God has allowed us to go through is for a reason. We might not see that reason at the time. We may stand up and scream at God, asking, "Why me, God? Why me?" The answers to this burning question and desire to know may not be apparent at the time. However brutally painful it might be, there will eventually be an answer.

That reminds me of a Beatles song my friends Todd George Stone and his partner Chris Weber sang so beautifully at my mother's funeral. It was "Let It Be."

By these famous lyrics, know that there will be an answer when you surrender to what is and just let it be. And by this, I don't mean to say just give up. No, never. Accept what is and recognize your own worth and worthiness, your own special God-given strength, and do whatever you need to do to love yourself enough to 'step up and into your power' to create a better outcome and future for yourself. You, and only you, can do it, and believe me, you are more capable of doing so than you may think. Be resilient; be strong!

None of us are immune to problems cropping up from time to time, some most unexpected when they hit you like a freight train coming out of nowhere. Don't ignore the blaring horns warning you in a second. What do all successful people have in common? They have a thought, which turns into an idea. They start to put a plan in place to do the work and then make that dream, that thought, manifest itself into reality. They see it in their mind's eye as already being real before it ever happens. These are the winners in the world, and you can be one of those people too. We're not lucky; we had to work for it. Some people say "work hard"; I say "work smarter." We have all learned and are still learning that trials will come, and trials will pass. It's all in how you respond to these challenges. When you fail, and you will, you get back up, dust yourself, and try again. It's by never giving up on yourself and never, ever giving up! Always remember it's never too late to start all over. It's never too late to show up and step up as the authentic you, but you must believe!

I'm also reminded of the well-known beloved and inspirational Disney movie I recently re-watched "The Lion King," where Simba the lion cub grows up through adversity, not believing in himself or ever feeling 'good enough.' He learns differently through his life by overcoming many challenges and really learning who he is. The story ends with the song "Never Too Late For Hope" and these final words: "Never forget who you are."

Books like these, written by some of those very people who had a dream, are written from the heart and soul to show you how and encourage you to know that if we can do it, so can you! And that's the truth, my friend. These authors left no stone unturned. It's all right here.

This is one of those books you will underline and mark the pages, leave on your desk or bedside table, and use as a reference manual when you want to refer back to something that was said. It will come in handy!

All of us are here to help you and are easily accessible if or when you need us. We are all here to serve you in any way we can.

A personal note from the originator and creator of the series which begins with this one: The second one is about creating joy through hope by rising over life's adversities. Look for it to come soon!

May God lead you and bless you through our words. We wish you the very best life has to offer. Grab it by the horns and make the best of it! You are love and dearly loved.

With sincere gratitude,

Char Murphy

## About Char Murphy

"Works done in service through hope, love, faith and gratitude for the good of humanity shall always be rewarded."

—*Char Murphy*

Char Murphy is an Attorney; International Best-Selling Author; Top Author Coach of the Year 2022; *Top Inspirational Author of the Year 2020;*

*SABA 2020 Book Awards Author Winner for "Unshakeable Power" - Through Seasons of the Soul."*

With more than three decades of professional experience, Char Murphy has certainly proven herself to be an *expert in multiple fields.* She's a *dynamic, results-driven passionate leader and change-agent, empowering mentor and advocate, business consultant, and strategist, life transformation to transitions guide.*

Her entrepreneurial spirit has given rise to several successful businesses -

*"Believeinspire With Char Murphy"; Next Level Writer's Academy; "Murphy's Law Firm."*

Although Ms. Murphy has received many accolades and awards on her journey back from darkness and despair - she considers her most meaningful and important accomplishments as being a pre-eminent supporter, mentor and advocate for helping people, supporting them in re-imagining their dreams and living their greatest joy.

Many seek Char's wisdom as a gifted, personable and relatable communicator. She graciously and joyfully accepts and embraces her social responsibility, with the opportunities presented to share her compelling story of survival and self re-discovery with individuals as well as the collective, especially during such pivotal times as now.

Char's passion is to encourage, empower and enlighten others using examples from her difficult life experiences to teach and show, how to maneuver through and beyond the many twists, sharp turns and roadblocks on the highway of life. Which eventually leads to positive change and transformation. She has a knowing that *"she's been blessed to bless and serve others- to give back what she's been given for the greater good of all."*

In her latest book, *"Unshakeable Power,"* Char delivers warm, engaging, dynamic, and insightful content. She uses her heartening journey of hardships and recovery through hope-healing, shift-transitions, grit-determination, and faith to overcome and pivot to a higher professional-personal mastery and achievement.

It's all about facing, dealing with, and overcoming limited beliefs about ourselves and facing the fears of illusions, which are not true.

Success is dependent and paramount upon learning to re-connect within yourself, reaching deep inside joining heart-mind, body-soul, to re-discover and reveal you-you've always been. To recognize, harness, step up and into your unique strengths, let go of the past to move ahead with personal resolve and self-confidence towards engaging with and implementing your true purpose.

Char put herself through law school as a single mom later in life, then after investing 15 years of dedication to her legal career, as a highly respected attorney, she was forced to retire due to the debilitating effects of four breast cancer diagnoses, many painful surgeries and exhausting treatments while juggling the duties of running her law firm. She not only lost her hard-earned career and successful law practice, but also her identity of *"who she thought she was."* She questioned who she was, why she was still here, and what she would do next. Growing up, Char endured parental abuse and abandonment, yet as a young adult, held her family together while providing primary support and healthcare at home to her father who suffered through and died from ALS. And later to her mother who died from Alzheimer's.

Her life story is a testament to her inner strength and ability to overcome these life altering circumstances. She turned her challenges into a positive life mission to encourage and be an inspirational influence to her audiences. She exemplifies and teaches others how to stand strong in their power - to have confidence, trust, faith and belief in themselves, moving forward. Char's transformational message is of beating the odds and thriving through seemingly endless transitions, knowing everything happens for a greater purpose.

In the words of Char Murphy *"I am grateful for everything and wouldn't change a thing."*

Please contact Char Murphy for group speaking engagements, retreats, summits, podcasts, ghostwriting, article writing, consulting, and personal mentoring. Also for her expert guidance in writing your own book, or writing/publishing your inspiring story in one of her upcoming anthologies, where authors and writers tell their stories to let you know, "you are not alone in your struggles." We have been where you are.

Look for more books to come in the *Mission Hope* series. Char's contact information below.

Blog and Website: believeinspire.us
Email: char@believeinspire.us
LinkedIn: Charlotte (Char) Murphy
Facebook Group: BelieveInspire with Char Murphy
Instagram: @believeinspirewithcharmurphy
Purchase *Unshakeable Power* on Amazon and Barnes & Noble

CPSIA information can be obtained
at www.ICGtesting.com
Printed in the USA
BVHW041411310323
661521BV00001B/66

9 781956 353426